Panama's Canal

What Happens When the United States Gives a Small Country What It Wants

Mark Falcoff

The AEI Press

Publisher for the American Enterprise Institute

WASHINGTON, D.C.

1998

Available in the United States from the AEI Press, c/o Publisher Resources Inc., 1224 Heil Quaker Blvd., P.O. Box 7001, La Vergne, TN 37086-7001. To order: 1-800-269-6267. Distributed outside the United States by arrangement with Eurospan, 3 Henrietta Street, London WC2E 8LU England.

Library of Congress Cataloging-in-Publication Data

Falcoff, Mark.
    Panama's Canal : what happens when the United States gives a small country what it wants / Mark Falcoff.
      p. cm.
    Includes bibliographic references and index.
    ISBN 0-8447-4030-6 (alk. paper). — ISBN 0-8447-4031-4 (pbk. : alk. paper)
    1. Panama Canal (Panama)—Politics and government. 2. Panama Canal Treaties (1977) 3. Panama—Politics and government—1981- 4. Panama—Social conditions. 5. Panama—Foreign relations—United States. 6. United States—Foreign relations—United States. I. Title.
F1569.C2F35 1998
327.7307287—dc21   98-14395
                                                  CIP

1 3 5 7 9 10 8 6 4 2

THE AEI PRESS
Publisher for the American Enterprise Institute
1150 17th Street, N.W., Washington, D.C. 20036

Printed in the United States of America

Panama's Canal

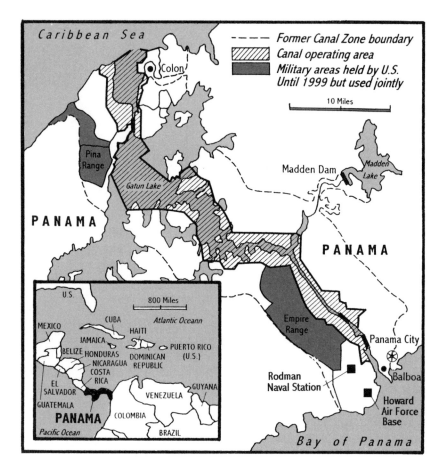

Former Canal Zone boundary
Canal operating area
Military areas held by U.S.
Until 1999 but used jointly

10 Miles

Caribbean Sea

Colon

Pina Range

Gatun Lake

PANAMA

Madden Dam

Madden Lake

PANAMA

Empire Range

Panama City

Balboa

Rodman Naval Station

Howard Air Force Base

Bay of Panama

U.S.

800 Miles

Atlantic Oceann

CUBA

MEXICO

HAITI

JAMAICA

BELIZE

HONDURAS

PUERTO RICO (U.S.)

DOMINICAN REPUBLIC

NICARAGUA

COSTA RICA

EL SALVADOR

GUYANA

VENEZUELA

GUATEMALA

PANAMA

COLOMBIA

Pacific Ocean

BRAZIL

Contents

Acknowledgments

The author acknowledges the generous support provided for this study by the Lynde and Harry Bradley Foundation.

Thanks are also due to his research assistant, Dean H. Schaffer, and to his executive assistant at the American Enterprise Institute, Gwendolyn Wilber.

Many U.S. government and military officials, past and present, have provided helpful comments on the manuscript. The author, however, has chosen to thank each of them individually and privately.

Panama's Canal

1

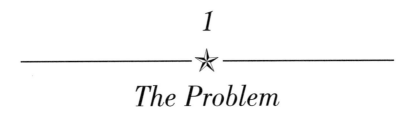

The Problem

Though most Americans are probably unaware of the fact, at the close of this century the Panama Canal will officially pass to the ownership of the Republic of Panama, and the American flag will cease to fly in the isthmus for the first time in more than ninety years. That an event of this moment hardly merits mention in our daily press is surely no accident, since the Carter-Torrijos treaties that established the transfer in 1978 purposely stretched the process out over more than two decades. This time lag was designed partly to defuse political opposition to the treaties in the United States at the time of ratification and also to give Panamanians a chance to work into their new role gradually.

In a purely technical sense, the process of devolution has been reasonably successful. None of the disasters predicted by opponents of the treaties in 1978 have come to pass—so far. In drafting the treaties, however, a remarkable number of crucial issues were ignored, postponed, or swept under the rug. Some of them are now poised to foist themselves on us. Meanwhile, something has happened that no one could have predicted—the end of the cold war and the disappearance of the Soviet Union as the principal adversary of the United States. As a result, the Republic of Panama has lost much of the room for maneuver that allowed it, despite its small size and vulnerability, to manipulate American and world politics in its favor at a specific point in historic time. These two anomalies form the basis of the present book.

To be sure, no treaty, no matter how brilliantly crafted, can foresee all possible contingencies, particularly over a period of more than two decades. The world changes every day. Nonetheless, quite a few of the problems faced by Panama as the future custodian of the canal were easily predictable in 1978, and indeed some of them were discussed quite authoritatively in the Senate hearings convened to examine the Carter-Torrijos accords. This point is underscored in chapter 2 by reopening the transcripts of those hearings; in chapter 4 the relevant issues and problems are carefully explored.

In contemplating the future of the canal—one of the world's most important transit routes—we need to bear in mind constantly that the treaty itself was concluded not with a mere geographical abstraction but with a specific political regime that governed a particular kind of country. With characteristic Wilsonian presumption, the Carter administration tried to ignore or minimize the distinctive features of Panamanian society and politics and to pretend that it was dealing with a state like any other. Nothing could be further from the truth. Panama was created by the United States to serve as host to the interoceanic route that it proposed to build; the country's sense of self has been almost entirely dependent on its relationship with the United States, both cooperative and adversarial; the exigencies of canal construction, on one hand, and the creation of a powerful commercial entrepôt, on the other, led to the importation or immigration of people of other countries and cultures. In some ways, this latter turn of events has created a formidable obstacle to the evolution of a coherent national identity.

Although the quality of Panamanian public life has significantly improved in recent years, the Carter administration concluded the canal treaties without any assurance that such would be the case by the time the year 2000 rolled around. Instead, although famously allergic to regimes of force elsewhere in the hemisphere, the Carter White House was forced into the embarrassing position of making excuses for one signal exception. Though the Torrijos dictatorship has long since disappeared, along with the military caste on which it was built, its enduring legacy to Panama is a political culture that fits rather uncomfortably within the framework of democratic customs and mores. As Panama prepares itself to assume a new and more independent role in international affairs, such institutions as it does possess could be described in the best of cases as tentative, even rickety. Chapter 3 unravels the country's complicated history and sociology, with a view to reminding readers that it will be Panama—not Switzerland, Luxembourg, or even Costa Rica—that will be running one of the world's major maritime facilities after the year 2000.

Some events of the 1980s in Panama—specifically, the collapse of a populist-nationalist consensus and the rise of General Manuel Noriega, climaxing in the U.S. invasion of 1989—led many Panamanians to doubt that in the long run the departure of the United States from their country best served their national interest. In many ways, they were not wrong, but the peculiar anomalies of Panamanian politics—a politics strangely insulated from the harsh realities of daily life of ordinary citizens but perfectly attuned to the sensibilities of the urban mob and the media—ensured that until recently almost no one would dare to say as much in public.

A curious game of hide-and-seek has resulted, with the Panamanian political class hoping against hope that the United States would beg to remain in the country under circumstances so self-effacing that the politicians could have it both ways—retain the economic, psychological, and political benefits of the American presence without having to admit that the entire enterprise of Panamanian nationalism was hollow at its core. Such an outcome would have served the Panamanian political class in another way as well: it would have retained the United States as a convenient whipping boy for all the deficiencies of Panamanian society, as well as an American garrison to reassure foreign investors and local elites, both perhaps understandably wary of the country's problematic political stability.

As explained in chapter 5, the changing international context since the end of the cold war has rendered this a virtual impossibility. Even the compromise agreement currently being negotiated between Panama and the United States—a multinational drug center that will allow a tiny complement of American troops to remain under the fig leaf of a fictitious multilateral authority—falls far short of what is needed, to satisfy either the Panamanian political or business classes, the American defense establishment, or the international shipping community. It is not even clear that the agreement, if it takes the form of a treaty to which the United States is a party, will win Senate approval. Even if it does, for reasons to be explained subsequently, the Panamanian public may yet reject the arrangement in a plebiscite to be held sometime in 1998.

The effective departure of American civil and military authority from the isthmus is bound to have weighty consequences. While no one can predict the future, some of the most prominent bumps on the road are clearly discernible. This book attempts to point them out for the benefit of all parties concerned.

At times, this book may seem excessively detailed. But, in writing it, I have purposely tried to counteract—with hard facts and figures—the expansive, not to say exaggerated, rhetoric of the current Panamanian government and, particularly, of the Regional Interoceanic Authority (ARI) and its director, Nicolás Ardito Barletta. I have also drawn extensively on the Panamanian media over the past decade to give readers some sense of the tone and texture of public debate, which at times has been remarkably frank and revealing.

In choosing so provocative a subtitle as *What Happens When the United States Gives a Small Country What It Wants*, I have perhaps made unjustified claims for this book. At the least, I probably should have put a question mark behind the phrase. After all, nobody knows exactly what will happen when the canal reverts to Panama, but the kinds of problems that it must face are now perfectly visible, and they do not encourage the artificial euphoria that informed the recent Universal Congress on the Canal (September 7–11, 1997). Rather, these difficulties invite Panamanians, and indeed anyone interested in their country, to serious and sober reflection.

This book, however, is not merely about Panama or a particular problem relating to its future. It is also a parable fraught with considerable meaning for other small countries, particularly those belonging to what we used to call the third world. As the twentieth century draws to a close, it is painfully obvious that the pyrotechnics of anti-imperialism, which illuminated our political and cultural skies for the four decades after World War II, provide but meager sustenance for non-Western societies the morning after decolonization. The point is *not* that such societies should seriously consider petitioning for a return to foreign domination, since that is impossible in any case, but rather that those who lead their people into the promised land of independence must be prepared to assume a new level of responsibility for their welfare. Every act of liberation carries with it a corresponding burden of responsibility. This is the point of chapter 6. One can only hope that Panama's leaders will understand this and act accordingly; they need merely to look about them at any meeting of the Nonaligned Movement to see what will happen to their country if they fail to do so. One hopes, that is, that Panama will not become—like Cuba, Algeria, Angola,

Vietnam, and other countries still intoxicated with the anti-imperialist dream—a dysfunctional society, continually opening old scabs, choking on yesterday's rhetoric, a threat only to itself, and, as such, a counterexample and warning to others.

The transfer of the canal and U.S. military properties to Panama is, then, an issue both ideological and concrete. In looking at what would seem to be a specific problem of a very small country, this book aspires to make a serious contribution to public policy. But it is intended as well to cast into sharp relief the particular problems facing many formerly colonial and dependent countries as we enter what might be called the post–anti-imperialist age.

2

★

The Treaties

A t noon on the last day of 1999, the Republic of Panama will come into full possession of the canal that bisects its territory, as well as all the adjacent lands and several billion dollars' worth of properties and improvements. In so doing, the country will complete a twenty-two-year process established by the Carter-Torrijos treaties of 1978, ratified by the U.S. Senate, and approved by the Panamanian people in a nationwide plebiscite. Thus will conclude an entire epoch of direct American presence in the circum-Caribbean, as well as nearly a century of quasi-colonial tutelage virtually coterminous with Panama's history as an independent nation.

By most standards, and certainly compared with Britain's debacle over Suez, the phased American withdrawal from Panama has proved thus far to be one of the more successful examples of recent imperial (or quasi-imperial) devolution in the postwar era. Despite deep emotions on both sides and the ever-present potential for violence, Panama and the United States managed to reach compromise on profoundly divisive issues. Moreover, despite dark predictions by many American residents in the Canal Zone and their allies in the U.S. political community, to date the transition to Panamanian management of the canal has proceeded in good order. Unfortunately, no treaty, no matter how well thought out, can make full provision for every eventuality, least of all for a period stretching across more than two decades. This book is basically about the dilemmas—many of them wholly unanticipated—

posed by changes in Panama, the United States, and the world since the Carter-Torrijos treaties were signed. The best place to start is with the documents themselves.

Not One Treaty but Two

At the negotiations, Panama's paramount interest was to wrest control of the canal and acquire (or reacquire) sovereignty over a ten-mile strip on either side, which had been governed as a U.S. territory since 1903. The overriding concern of the United States was to assure itself that, in meeting these Panamanian demands, its own security interests would be respected and assured. Although neither side could abandon its minimal negotiating position, the process itself rested on the assumption that Panamanian and U.S. objectives were not ultimately incompatible. As far as the drafters were concerned, there was no necessary contradiction. But, in the end, accommodating both agendas required drafting two different instruments.[1]

The first establishes the rules and procedures for devolution. It recognizes for the first time Panama's ultimate sovereignty over the entire isthmus, while establishing that during the transition period the United States would have the right to "manage, operate, maintain, improve, and protect and defend the Canal." At the same time, the United States pledges to facilitate increasing Panamanian participation "in the management and protection and defense of the Canal." This document creates a new body known as the Panama Canal Commission, composed of nine members—five U.S. nationals and four Panamanians—"proposed by the Republic of Panama for appointment to such positions by the United States of America in a timely manner" (Articles 1 and 3).

Section 3(b) of Article 3 establishes in rather vague terms a procedure for the replacement of such Panamanian members of the board as might prove (for whatever reason) unacceptable to the United States. This section stipulates that from the time the treaties enter into force and until January 1, 1990, the administrator of the canal would be an American citizen, while the deputy would be a Panamanian national. Thereafter, their positions would reverse. "Such Panamanian nationals shall be proposed [for this position] to the United States of America by the Republic of Panama for appointment to such positions by the United States of America." These rather innocuous provisions were based on the presumption that correct and cordial relations between the two governments would invariably prevail. As this proved incorrect, these provisions were the germs of the U.S. military intervention in December 1989.

This first treaty also formally abolishes the Canal Zone Government and the Panama Canal Company, turning over to the Republic of Panama the responsibility for "services of a general jurisdictional nature"—in other words, postal services, customs and immigration, courts and licensing (Article 3, section 6). For the duration of the transition period, however, the United States retains "primary responsibility to protect and defend the Canal." This includes the right to "station, train and move military forces within the Republic of Panama." A joint military commission (the Combined Board) was created to advise on this mission and to plan for contingencies (Article 4, sections 1–5).

This initial agreement also recognizes that the construction of a sea-level canal may become necessary to meet the needs of international navigation and that both parties commit themselves to studying this possibility. The United States specifically obligates itself not to negotiate with third parties on this subject without the explicit approval of the Republic of Panama. For its part, Panama grants to the United States the right to add a third lane of locks "at any time during the duration of this Treaty" (Article 12, sections 1–3).

Finally, the treaty provides for the eventual transfer of "all real property and non-removable improvements" in the former Canal Zone, including the Panama Railroad. In the meanwhile, the government of Panama will be paid a portion of the canal operating revenues fixed at U.S. $0.30 per Panama Canal net ton for each vessel transiting the canal, to be adjusted biennially to take into account changes in the U.S. consumer price index. The Republic of Panama is guaranteed a fixed annuity of U.S. $10 million per year and another amount—up to an additional U.S. $10 million—to be paid out of canal operating expenses "to the extent that such revenues exceed expenditures." If operating revenues in any given year do not produce a surplus to cover this payment, compensation will be drawn from operating surpluses in future years (Article 13, sections 1–4).

The second treaty is far shorter and deals with the permanent neutrality and operation of the canal during and after the transitional period. The document was drafted to meet the concerns of those in the United States who regarded the Republic of Panama as a doubtful repository of its long-term security and commercial interests. The latter pledges to keep the waterway open in both peace and war to "transit by the vessels of all nations on terms of entire equality" so that the Isthmus of Panama "shall not be the target of reprisals in any armed conflict between other nations of the world." After the termination of the first treaty, "only the Republic of Panama shall operate the Canal and maintain military forces, defense sites, and military installations within its national territory." In recognition of the original U.S. role in developing the waterway, however, and given its close historic relationship with the Republic of Panama, in time of war U.S. vessels will be entitled to transit the canal "expeditiously," which has generally been interpreted to mean that in emergency circumstances its naval bottoms would move to the head of the line.

The Road to Carter-Torrijos

Although Panamanians toyed with the notion of autonomy—if not outright secession from Colombia—throughout the nineteenth century, the creation of an independent republic out of a breakaway province was the work of an American president. Weary of exhausting and apparently unrewarding negotiations for a transisthmian route with the government in Bogotá, President Theodore Roosevelt actively connived and conspired with Panamanian and Panamanian-based foreign adventurers to bring about a new state with which he could do business. Almost from the day of its creation, however, the Republic of Panama had a less than satisfactory relationship with its new protector. In exchange for the right to build, operate, and fortify the canal and to establish an American presence in what became the Canal Zone, Panama received U.S. $10 million plus an annual annuity of $250,000. In exchange, foreigners ended up controlling some 550 square miles of the new country's best real estate, "including the nation's prime deepwater locations and potentially profitable commercial opportunities in the Zone, from which Panamanians were excluded."[2]

The presence of a privileged American military and civilian community in what amounted to an extraterritorial enclave (in some ways the equivalent of the treaty ports in China) was a constant goad to resentment and ill-feeling; from 1924 onward, anti-American violence periodically erupted. Unsurprisingly, although the original Hay–Bunau Varilla Treaty (1903) granted the concession to the United States in perpetuity, from the 1930s one can perceive a discernible trend toward revision in a direction favorable to Panama. Under the Hull-Alfaro agreements (1936), for example, the United States raised the annual annuity to U.S. $430,000, and renounced the right to intervene unilaterally in Panama to defend the canal or Panama's independence. The United States also surrendered the right to acquire additional territory for the canal. In theory at least, this ended Panama's status as an American protectorate.

A Treaty of Mutual Cooperation and Understanding (1955) increased the annual payment to the government of Panama to U.S. $2 million, provided greater access to the zone for Panamanian businesses, and ceded property outside the zone, estimated at approximately U.S. $4 million. The agreement also established the principle of the same basic wage for all Canal Zone employees regardless of nationality. Five years later, after prolonged negotiation, the United States agreed to allow the flags of both nations to fly alongside each other at the same height in one designated spot within the zone (extended to all flag sites in 1963). At the same time, the United States agreed to allow the use of Panamanian postage stamps within the zone.

The concession on flags produced a boisterous response on the part of American students at Balboa High School in the zone; they ran up the U.S. flag without its required Panamanian companion just after New Year's Day 1964. What began as a childish prank in deplorable taste acquired the proportions of a major international incident: a group of Panamanian students, marching into the zone to register their indignation, got mixed up with a mob of adults that had apparently assembled over a pending labor dispute. Agitators went to work; in short order Panama City was rocked by bloodcurdling demonstrations, looting, and random violence. Panama broke off diplomatic relations with the United States, and they were only renewed at the end of the year in exchange for informal assurances of major new concessions by the United States.

In many of its essentials, the agreement reached between Presidents Lyndon B. Johnson and Marco Robles in September 1965 foreshadows Carter-Torrijos. The former committed both countries to replacing the 1903 treaty with a new document that would recognize Panama's sovereignty over the zone; it acknowledged that the replacement for Hay–Bunau Varilla would likewise expire after a certain number of years or on the opening of a second Panama Canal (if the United States chose to build one) and that the United States would maintain military bases in Panama to safeguard its security interests in the immediate area. For the first time, U.S. troops in Panama operated under a status of forces agreement such as the agreements that governed their presence in other major treaty countries such as Italy, Germany, and France.

Within the framework of this agreement, negotiators from both sides labored for over two years on a draft treaty that would effectively transfer the waterway to Panama. In a development that in many ways anticipated the controversy provoked by Carter-Torrijos, however, before negotiations could be completed, its import was leaked to the press and caused an immediate political sensation. Already embroiled in an extremely problematic relationship with his own party over the Vietnam War, President Johnson decided to postpone signing the draft treaty until after the 1968 U.S. elections. The Panamanians chose to interpret this postponement as a personal rebuff and immediately declared that they no longer regarded the existing draft as an acceptable basis for negotiation.

By this time, the movement for a drastic revision of the Panamanian-U.S. status quo was overwhelming, so much so that even the administration of President Richard Nixon (1969–1975) showed no signs of wishing to resist it. Indeed, the principles worked out in complicated discussions between National Security Adviser (later Secretary of State) Henry Kissinger and Panamanian Foreign Minister Juan Tack became the skeleton of the Carter-Torrijos treaties.

The Treaty Controversy

From the perspective of the late 1990s, it is easy to pick out these episodes in treaty revision as the main features of the historical landscape. Or perhaps the road to Carter-Torrijos seems obvious in retrospect, with recognizable markers laid down over a long period of time that should have made the ultimate destination clear to all and sundry. Yet such was not the case. Instead, when the full import of the canal treaties became apparent to the U.S. public, an unexpected grass-roots political movement nearly succeeded in getting the Senate to reject them. As it was, that body eventually ratified the documents by a single vote, even though General Omar Torrijos, the Panamanian president-dictator, had threatened—with characteristic hyperbole—to disable the canal with dynamite charges if the U.S. Senate refused its approval.

Just why the Carter-Torrijos treaties became the most controversial foreign policy issue to divide the Senate and American public since the Treaty of Versailles is a fascinating question. On the evidence, most Americans appear to have been wholly unaware of the negotiations that led up to the canal treaties; for all we can know, the majority may have long assumed that the arrangements laid down in Hay–Bunau

Varilla had never been subject to revision. If so, the sudden announcement by President Carter of the new dispensation must have come as a shock. Many Americans had served in the zone during and after World War II, and the canal itself was a monument to American technology, know-how, and determination to succeed in a physically hostile environment. Generations of American politicians and military officers had emphasized the centrality of the canal and the zone to U.S. security concerns; no meeting of any of the large veterans' organizations was complete without a ritual tip of the hat to this notion. Indeed, much U.S. foreign policy in the circum-Caribbean for the first half of the twentieth century was organized around the principle of protecting the canal or its access routes, which, in practice, provided an all-purpose rationale (whether well- or ill-founded) for intervening in Cuba, the Dominican Republic, Haiti, and Nicaragua.[3] Moreover, the troubled political life of Panama itself did not inspire much confidence, to say the least, in the capacity of the country to administer this uniquely American institution responsibly.[4]

The treaty controversy also had a cultural dimension, however difficult to pin down in precise terms. Had President Richard Nixon been in office during the period 1977–1981, it is just possible that the divisive campaign for ratification might have been avoided—or at least greatly moderated. This much is suggested, at least, by Nixon's proven capacity to package controversial foreign policy initiatives (such as the opening to China) in the language of assertive nationalism, as well as his enduring influence with some of the most conservative sectors of the U.S. electorate. The Carter administration, however, saw the treaties not as merely one more item on its foreign policy agenda but rather as the centerpiece of an entirely new approach to world politics. Its common denominator, as the former deputy White House chief of staff has written, was "repudiation of containment, of policies based on ideology and traditional spheres of influence."[5]

Carter's Latin American policy was based (according to the same authoritative source) on "righting old wrongs: normalizing relations with Cuba and with such other leftist regimes in the hemisphere as Jamaica and Guyana, inaugurating long-needed human rights initiatives," and treating other nations as sovereign—in other words, "placing U.S. policy on the side of history."[6] Surrender of the canal and the zone to Panama was just the beginning; to follow would be new policies toward Rhodesia and South Africa, as well as Vietnam, with which the president intended to normalize relations, and South Korea, where he contemplated a significant drawdown of U.S. troop strength.[7] Quite a few Americans, by no means all of them conservatives, did not share the view that the United States had been on the wrong side of history and, when the canal treaties were presented as one method of rectification, reacted strongly.

General Torrijos professed to be convinced that President Carter felt a genuine sense of shame for America's record in world affairs. Indeed, it was one of the weapons that he brandished in his own domestic campaign to win support for the treaties in a national plebiscite. In a television address fortunately not widely reproduced in the United States (though made available to members of the U.S. Senate), he explained to his people that

> when I talk with Carter I realize that I am talking [with] a man who has turned his back on intervention, that I am facing a man of high moral character....
>
> He was elected in a country [whose inhabitants] felt a certain moral loathing because their fatherland, the United States, had turned into the world's international policeman, because they have young people on their way back from interventions, because it is a youth which feels moral loathing and repugnance for what happened in Santo Domingo, for what happened in Vietnam and for what happened in Playa Girón [the Bay of Pigs].... It is a country on its way back from such interventions, and he did not want [them] for a single moment....
>
> He told me: Have faith, have faith because moral causes always prevail. Your cause is moral and so is my attitude in listening to a moral attitude. I know I am capable of convincing my people that they have been taught a distorted [version of] history and that, as a result of this, many of them have come to feel that Panama exists under the same moral or geographical condition as Alaska or Louisiana, but that is my problem and I can assure that I can resolve that problem....
>
> What has happened is that a series of circumstances arose in which the correlation of force was a correlation of moral forces, because a President Carter emerged who is ashamed to apply force to a weak country, who feels shame and listens to his country's youth who do not want to return to the battlefields of Vietnam.[8]

Torrijos may have wildly exaggerated the content of his private conversations with President Carter. But unquestionably both sides saw themselves as engaged in an exercise of historical reparation. For President Carter, certainly the spirit, if not the precise letter, of these remarks pervaded most of his major foreign policy pronouncements. But most Americans did not feel that their country's failure in Vietnam was due to a lack of moral rectitude or that the incapacity to oust the Castro regime in Cuba at the Bay of Pigs was a stain on American honor (except insofar as President Kennedy refused to provide the invaders with adequate air cover), less still that their country's presence in Panama for three-quarters of a century should properly inspire a sense of shame. Possibly, even with a different sort of ideological packaging the treaties would have had a difficult time in winning approval from the Senate and U.S. public. But the particular cultural reference points employed by the Carter administration made the task of its opponents immeasurably easier.

The Future As Seen in 1978

Quite apart from the idiosyncratic perspective of their principal signatories, the treaties cannot be understood without some reference to the era in which they were drafted. They coincided with a period of declining American self-confidence, whose leitmotifs were the collapse of client-states in Vietnam and Cambodia, a dramatic rise in oil prices followed by unprecedented inflation, the decline of the dollar, and a program of massive rearmament in the Soviet Union, which provoked new currents of neutrality and pacifism among America's traditional allies in Western Europe. Above all, the 1970s were the golden age of nonalignment in what was then called the third world, as exemplified by the tendency of small countries to cluster together into anti-Western (and usually anti-U.S.) coalitions at the United Nations and other international bodies.

The Carter administration—and to some extent its most immediate predecessors—accepted as a given that the unquestioned hegemony of the United States in world affairs, which Americans had assumed since the end of World War II, had come to an end. The name of the game for American diplomacy became, as President Carter's national security adviser Zbigniew Brzezinski subsequently put it in the characteristic language of the time, "to develop more accommodating North-South relations, political as well as economic, so as to develop greater economic stability and growth in the Third World, diminish hostility toward the U. S., lessen Soviet influence, and increase the stake those nations would have in good relations with the North and the West."[9]

Critics of Carter's Latin American policy were later to argue that a policy of accommodation to (or appeasement of) emerging new forces in the region amounted to capitulation to enemies both near and far.[10] As things turned out, this was certainly so in Nicaragua and (but for the election of Ronald Reagan in 1980) might well have become so in El Salvador. In the particular case of Panama, however, Carter's contrafactual assumption—namely, that by abdicating direct control of the canal and by ceding the zone, U.S. interests would be more, not less, secure—turned out to be true in the short and (so far) middle run, though not because the world was supposedly being reshaped into a more egalitarian place, ruled by one state–one vote. (This is a point that we return to later.)

Of course, world history seen from Panama around 1978 took on an entirely different coloration. The willingness of the United States to sign the treaties was interpreted as proof positive that the balance of power in world politics had shifted to the smaller nonaligned states, and, in truth, Torrijos had done an excellent job of lobbying on his country's behalf—at the United Nations, the Nonaligned Movement, and the Organization of American States. He had traveled widely and enlisted the support of foreign leaders as diverse as Venezuela's President Carlos Andrés Pérez and Yugoslavia's President Tito. To the extent that these factors contributed to the atmospherics, they may well have done much to shape the approach of the Carter administration, which was extremely solicitous of such organizations and took them quite seriously. Yet, in the end, the position of the United States was inspired less by pressures from the Nonaligned Movement or even the Organization of American States than by its own failure of nerve—its perception of itself as a fallen great power whose task was to manage its decline as gracefully as possible.

Less sophisticated circles in Panama had understandably little or no interest in the international implications of the treaties. Rather, the promised transfer of the canal and the zone was seen as a miracle that would transform the country virtually overnight, raising its living standard to the level of the leading industrial nations. Indeed, it is not impossible that many Panamanians thought that the power and prosperity of the United States were due precisely and perhaps even exclusively to its control of the canal.

Although at least 36 percent of those Panamanians who voted in the 1978 plebiscite rejected the treaties, it must be assumed that most of these did so because they felt that the arrangements were excessively generous to the United States or were at least disappointed that the transfer was spread out over so long a period. Certainly, if there were those who opposed the treaties because they wished to see a permanent American presence in Panama, they were all but invisible at the time.

Ratification Issues

In the U.S. Senate, the treaties were forced to run the gauntlet of a lengthy ratification process extending over many weeks and involving dozens of witnesses drawn from all walks of American life, including representatives of the U.S. community in the zone. The transcripts and accompanying documentation fill five substantial volumes of small type. Seven major issues were raised during these hearings. The first was *toll rates*. Since its opening in 1914, the canal had been operated by the U.S. government as a public facility for international shipping rather than as a profit-making enterprise. In many fiscal years after World War II, tolls could not cover the cost of maintenance, and the difference was made up by a direct appropriation by the U.S. Congress. This reality was greatly at variance with popular perceptions within Panama itself, where the canal was regarded as something of a golden goose. Raising the question of whether a realistic toll structure would prevail once the transfer was complete was therefore logical.

The second issue was *human rights and the quality of the Panamanian political process*. While by no means as repressive as some Latin American dictators of the day, General Torrijos could hardly be regarded as a democrat. He had come to power by a military coup; he had never held elections; his National Assembly was a rubber stamp; numerous opponents were exiled. He operated well within the tradition of Latin American personalism, however, and without doubt was genuinely popular. The nature of the Panamanian regime would not normally have raised problems for the United States—Torrijos was arguably no worse than many other leaders in the region, with few of whom Washington had experienced difficulty doing business—except that the Carter administration had made human rights so conspicuous a centerpiece of its policies elsewhere in Latin America. Torrijos was therefore something of an embarrassment. Administration witnesses were forced into some extremely strange convolutions to minimize or explain away problems in Panama that they had no trouble properly identifying in Chile, Argentina, Uruguay, Guatemala, El Salvador, and Nicaragua.

Senatorial critics and members of the U.S. conservative community generally made much of Torrijos's close friendship with Cuban dictator Fidel Castro, though, in fact, such affinity was grounded far less on ideology or strategic alignment than on a momentary convergence of interests and a characteristically Latin penchant for self-dramatization. (Both thought of themselves as world historic figures and were not shy about reminding others of the fact.) More serious were allegations of drug trafficking by Torrijos's brother, a charge that the State Department and the White House tended to treat as a red herring, whether disinterestedly or not. In the event, neither accusation proved particularly debilitating.

More troubling than Torrijos's behavior and his treatment of his domestic opponents was the question of political succession in Panama. No one doubted that Torrijos's signature was sufficient to guarantee respect for its treaty obligations as long as he was on the scene, but as Senator Joseph Biden asked Ambassador William Jorden, "What happens after the General goes? God forbid, suppose he is killed in an accident tomorrow ... won't there be a scrambling for power if something happens to Torrijos?"[11] (As it turned out, Senator Biden was remarkably prescient, since Torrijos died in a mysterious plane crash in July 1981, and his disappearance did indeed deprive Panamanian politics of its center of gravity.) Although Torrijos's presence as a strong, popular figure was a comfort to the Carter administration—to the extent that, once determined on a course, he could "deliver"—his problematic relationship with Panama's rickety or nonexistent political institutions raised questions about the kind of partner the United States would be dealing with more than twenty years later.

The third issue was the *neutrality treaty*, specifically what residual rights it granted to the United States. In effect, this second treaty was intended to soften up American opinion by providing an escape clause: nothing could go wrong in Panama because the United States could simply exercise its legal option to set things to rights. What this treaty did and did not authorize was the subject of variant interpretations in the United States and Panama. The Carter administration, which harbored no expectation of ever having to invoke the neutrality treaty, nonetheless assured critics that the agreement provided as wide a range of options as might ever be needed, while its opponents tended to exaggerate the restraining effects of the treaty's legalisms or its ambiguous phraseology. In the end, the administration was forced to accept a reservation drafted by Senator Dennis DeConcini that in specific terms reserved to the United States the right to unilateral intervention if and when it saw fit.[12]

DeConcini's reservation was a bitter pill for the Panamanian government to swallow. The Carter people finally succeeded in convincing their opposite numbers in Panama that there was no chance whatever of winning ratification without it. Some members of Torrijos's cabinet tried to defuse attacks at home from extreme nationalists and the Left, for whom the treaties—with or without the DeConcini amendment— were a sellout, by pointing out that what Panama on a piece of paper allowed the United States to do hardly mattered. In the final analysis, if the United States was hellbent on intervening, it would do so anyway, and not much could be done to stop it.[13] This prediction proved to be remarkably accurate.

The fourth issue was *alternatives to the treaties*, or what would happen if the Senate refused ratification. In many ways the administration's strongest argument was that there really was no alternative; having gone this far, the United States could not fall back without provoking a massive crisis in its relations not only with Panama but with the entire American continent. As Brzezinski puts it in his memoirs, "It was generally felt that violence would then ensue, and every intelligence assessment pointed to the likelihood that it would spread to other parts of Central America" and indeed beyond it.[14] Opponents of ratification were in the impossible position of having to prove that assessment was not true.

The fifth issue concerned the *environment*. By today's standards this subject got rather short shrift in the hearings, though two or three witnesses raised pregnant questions. In dispute was not merely the survival of certain species of wildlife, but the assurance of adequate supplies of fresh water for Panama City, where almost half the country's population now resides. The hearings also revealed that, without proper management of the ecosystem around Lake Gatún, the capacity of the canal to accommodate its normal flow of seaborne traffic would be imperiled.[15]

The sixth issue was the *popular reaction to the treaties in Panama and Latin America*. The administration was at pains to emphasize that *in Panama* the treaties were regarded as a compromise rather than an outright victory over the United States, since the conventional nationalist position there was that the canal and zone should be surrendered without delay. This was true—as far as it went. But, as some representatives of the U.S. community in the zone explained to the senators, Panamanian nationalism was not a profound phenomenon, and the appearance of unanimity on the subject of the treaties was somewhat deceptive.[16] While these witnesses were at times self-serving to a fault, they did show a deeper understanding of the dynamics of Panamanian politics than any administration witness—including U.S. Ambassador William Jorden—dared. Torrijos's decisive victory in the plebiscite, however, made the issue of Panamanian support for the treaties a moot point.

At official levels and in public forums, Latin American support for Panama's position was unanimous. Some countries on the South American West Coast (Ecuador, Chile, and Peru), strongly dependent on the canal for markets in Western Europe and the East Coast of the United States, however, were known to harbor misgivings about a Panamanian-controlled waterway. There was particular concern over the possibly irresponsible increases in canal tolls and the misallocation of funds earmarked for maintenance to other purposes—apprehensions inspired by firsthand knowledge of how publicly administered facilities operated in their own countries. None of this could be discussed authoritatively in the Senate hearings, since no Latin American figure was willing to declare such doubts or reservations.[17]

The seventh concern was the *geopolitical impact of the treaties on U.S. power.* The most vigorous case against ratification was laid out by Hanson Baldwin, the military editor of the *New York Times*, who was not actually a witness but whose treatise on the subject was inserted into the congressional record of the hearings. Baldwin's argument consisted of stacking a series of plausible (but far from inevitable) worst-case scenarios one against the other. "U.S. control and U.S. influence in this vital backdoor area—already impaired by the extension of Communist power and influence outward from Cuba ... would be fatally weakened," he concluded. "We cannot insure control without sovereignty.... We cannot provide military security for the canal without sovereignty; to attempt it would be to accept responsibility without authority."[18] The administration was easily able to counter Baldwin's logic with the cogent argument that a canal surrounded by a sullen, hostile population—and one led by a charismatic leader to boot—could hardly enhance U.S. security, all the more so since it would require the diversion of a far larger number of troops to protect it than if the treaties were to became law.

The End of "History"

To leaf through the transcripts of the Senate hearings on ratification is a bit like doing spadework on an archaeological dig, since the process uncovers layer after layer of a world utterly unlike the one in which we live today. In the years since 1978, the cold war has come to an end. There is no Soviet Union, and, with its disappearance, the whole concept of nonalignment has lost its meaning. The notion of a new international economic order, leveling differences between rich countries and poor, large powers and small, has been replaced by a new race for competitiveness and the rediscovery of comparative advantage. With the United States left as the world's sole remaining superpower, the Latin American agenda has shifted from trying to gain greater independence from it to winning access to its markets—the world's largest—and working out preferential trade and investment agreements with it.

This new context forces Panama to confront an extremely problematic geopolitical situation. Until 1978, its relationship to the United States broadly resembled that of Mexico. Both countries nursed deep historic and territorial grievances against the United States, but because both shared a common border (in Panama's case, the zone), they were advantageously placed in the broad strategic scheme of things. As such, each was in a position to demand high-priority treatment from the White House and State and Defense Departments.

Ownership of the canal and certain historic connections assure Panama that, at least for the immediate future, it will be something more than just another Latin American country for the United States. But once fully consummated, the Carter-Torrijos treaties will virtually end the "special relationship," a point that Panamanian officials and politicians have habitually overlooked. Meanwhile, the movement toward regional trade agreements has put Panama in a difficult position. Though a geographical extension of the Central American Isthmus, Panama blows hot and cold on whether it wishes to be considered part of the Central American community of nations.[19] Its reluctance to join the Central American Common Market puts it outside pending negotiations for parity with the North American Free Trade Area—that is, access to the combined free trade area of Mexico, Canada, and the United States created in 1993—though it is difficult to imagine that Panama will ever be regarded as important enough to win a treaty in its own right. (This situation may explain Panama's recent decision to join the Andean Community, ill-counseled to say the least, since for various reasons this bloc will probably be among the last group of states invited into the Free Trade Area of the Americas.) As it is, Panama's economy is highly protectionist; Panama was the last country to join the new World Trade Organization.

Insofar as the canal is concerned, whatever major strategic apprehensions its transfer might have inspired in the United States have lost their foundation. There is no competing superpower against which the canal must be protected, and even Castro's Cuba—deprived of its Soviet sponsor—has lost its bite. The region is not immune from other sorts of security threats, though none of the kind anticipated a quarter-century earlier. Meanwhile, nearly twenty years of joint operation with increasing Panamanian management have demonstrated thus far that there is no reason to fear precipitous increases in tolls or massive neglect of the physical infrastructure. To be sure, these propositions will be put to the test only once the last Americans have left. Already certain complaints about the tight-fisted way in which the Canal Commission is operating can be discerned in the background noise of Panamanian domestic politics, along with the reluctance of the current Pérez Balladares administration to use canal revenues for patronage purposes.

Of the seven issues raised during the ratification hearings, only two are at all relevant on the eve of transfer. One is the persistent weakness of Panama's political institutions; the other has to do with the environment, particularly as it impinges on both the urban water supply and the proper operation of the canal. Meanwhile, issues not contemplated either in the treaties or during the ratification debates have cropped up. One concerns the defense of the canal. The treaties assign this responsibility to the Panamanian military, but since the U.S. invasion of 1989, the Panamanian Defense Forces have been dismantled and replaced by a national police. Whatever the latter's deficiencies— and they are many—no one anticipates the early reconstitution of a Panamanian army, since its very existence is now prohibited by organic law.

The disappearance of the Panamanian military leaves the U.S. defense establishment in a curious position. Until the year 2000, it is the only other possible formation with legal, that is, treaty, rights to a military presence in the country. After that, Panama is left without any serious defense capability, somewhat like neighboring Costa Rica— with the important difference that the latter does not possess a strategic facility of international importance. This anomaly has raised the question of a residual U.S. base presence after 2000, an eventuality that is not prohibited by Carter-Torrijos, though it would obviously require an entirely new treaty. Since the abolition of the Panamanian Defense Forces, Panamanian public opinion has been increasingly friendly to this notion, as have some elements within the U.S. Departments of State and Defense. Such a development would require a major shift in policy by both countries and carries with it serious costs, benefits, and risks.

The second remaining point is the land and properties ceded by the United States to the Republic of Panama. These properties, commonly referred to as reverted areas, are situated in the old zone and amount to the largest single state-to-state transfer of land and improvements in the Western Hemisphere since at least the Chilean acquisition of the Peruvian provinces of Tacna and Arica in 1870. In dispute is Panama's need to absorb and readapt these properties to other uses. Although a special body, the Regional Interoceanic Authority (ARI) has been set up to plan for this contingency, so far Panama has not demonstrated much capacity to convert these facilities to productive use. The temptation to sell them off to foreign investors, including agencies controlled by governments outside the Western Hemisphere, has raised new and troubling questions about Panama's relationships.

The Carter-Torrijos treaties are therefore being superseded by history, not by "history." The Panamanians' realization that the United States does intend to leave and that they will find themselves alone in a world unlike the one their leaders anticipated more than twenty years ago has unleashed a serious, far-reaching, and soul-searching debate about the country, its institutions, and its real possibilities in the international economic order. Such questions are on the current agenda of all Latin American countries. But, except for Castro's Cuba, none must make decisions as radical in design, serious in purpose, and traumatic in emotional terms as Panama. That such decisions have been continually postponed since ratification of the treaties only underscores the drama and raises the potential costs of failure.

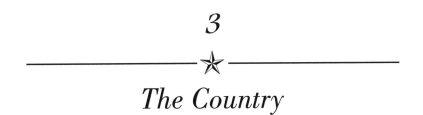

3

The Country

Panama's role in world affairs has been shaped since the sixteenth century by its advantageous geographical position, a narrow bridge between the two oceans and a crucial transit point between the North and South American continents. It was a major trading center even in the days of the Spanish Empire, when for a time it was the third richest colony in the New World. Nor is the notion of improving on nature particularly new: the Spanish monarchs seriously contemplated excavating a transisthmian canal as early as the 1500s. A railroad across the country's narrow waist was completed as early as 1850. Ferdinand de Lesseps, the builder of the Suez Canal, undertook to replicate his achievement in Panama in 1879 but was forced to abandon the project ten years later because of disease, engineering difficulties, and inadequate financing. De Lesseps's heirs and investors were eventually bought out by the U.S. government, which concluded an agreement with the infant Republic of Panama in 1903 to build the present canal.

"Geography Is Destiny"

The existence of the canal has merely accentuated, albeit radically, certain features of Panamanian society that have been present for a very long time. Unique among nations of the region, Panama is a curious combination of the provincial and international. Even for a Latin

American country, its society is extraordinarily diverse, culturally, racially, and linguistically. Despite efforts to develop other lines of endeavor, transoceanic shipping is the most important industry in the country, a fact underlined by its peculiar pattern of physical settlement. The most significant focus of urban development follows the path of the old Canal Zone, from Colón on the Atlantic side to Panama City on the Pacific (see map, frontispiece). Over time, the attraction of the canal and its associated activities have gradually altered the country's human geography; whereas in 1960 about one-third of the country's population lived in cities, by 1995 the urban population slightly exceeded 55 percent.[1]

Among other things, the presence of the canal and a large (until quite recently) U.S. military establishment in the zone have meant that Panama enjoyed a rather higher standard of living than most of its neighbors. Its annual per capita income, which was nearly $2,400 in 1995, is among the highest in the developing world. All the social indicators—per capita income, literacy, percentage of high school graduates, number of live births per thousand, proportion of the population engaged in nonagricultural occupations, life expectancy, and birth rate—place Panama closer to the upper-middle-class Latin American nations such as Argentina, Uruguay, and Venezuela than to, say, Nicaragua, El Salvador, and even neighboring Costa Rica. Critics are quick to point out—and they are right—that the numbers, however impressive in themselves, mask sharp inequalities between urban and rural areas and within social classes and groups in the capital and other cities.

During the colonial period, most of the population was of mixed Spanish-Indian descent (mestizos), though significant complements of Indians and even small numbers of African blacks rounded out the picture. Chinese indentured laborers were introduced during the building of the Panama railroad in the late 1840s, followed by large numbers of West Indian (or Antillean) blacks, Protestant and English-speaking, during construction of the canal in the first decade of the present century. The creation of a large commercial entrepôt, both in Panama City and in Colón, where a free zone was established, has attracted immigration from everywhere; Panama possesses visible and vigorous Jewish, Syrian-Lebanese, Greek, South Asian, and Western European communities. It is even home to several thousand American families who are retired from service in either the U.S. military or the old Panama Canal Company.

For many years, politics in Panama was controlled by a handful of well-to-do traditional families, often referred to as the oligarchy. Generally speaking, these people were recognizably of Spanish descent (therefore "white"), trained in a profession (usually law or medicine), and fluent in other languages, especially English, which they typically learned in the United States, often as college students. In the most literal sense of the word, these people were (and are) cosmopolitan; today they are equally at home in Madrid, Paris, New York, and Miami, where many also maintain homes. Not a few are married to Americans or Europeans. They have a broad knowledge of the wider world, which makes them ideal intermediators between their country and the great powers, particularly the United States, whose physical presence in Panama has been largely confined to diplomatic and military personnel on temporary assignment.

The degree to which this oligarchy has identifiable boundaries can be exaggerated; as a matter of fact, it has proved remarkably porous to new influences and members over the years. Conversely, to pick up a Panamanian newspaper is to be struck by the recurrence of the same last names—Arias, Arosemena, Alemán, Chiari, Goytía, de la Guardia, Lewis, Morgan, Vallarino—and not just in the society pages. This suggests that a recognizable, privileged elite is not merely a figment of some demagogue's imagination. Even putatively populist *caudillos* such as General Omar Torrijos and his unsavory successor, General Manuel Noriega—self-advertised scourges of the oligarchy—have not been reluctant to make use of those of its members whose services they required.

Panama possesses a rather large middle class for the region, largely mestizo in racial makeup but also including descendants of West Indian blacks, Chinese indentured laborers, Jews, recent immigrants from the Levant or South Asia, and some members of aristocratic families fallen on hard times. These people tend to be small businessmen, professionals, government administrators, and managerial and technical personnel. As a whole, this group places enormous emphasis on education and often makes enormous sacrifices to send its children to the university. It has provided much of the leadership and many of the shock troops of Panamanian populism, which is not surprising given that, as a class, it has depended heavily on government employment. (First-generation immigrants tend to depart from this stereotype; most are concerned with commerce and tend to be conservative or even passive in politics.)

The lower classes in Panama are divided by geography and means of livelihood, as well as race, language, and religion. In the countryside, the major component is the peasantry, subdivided into Indian and Hispanic (actually, mixed race) communities. In the cities, the picture is more complex still: it comprehends both skilled and semiskilled workers, as well as employees of the canal and the former zone. The latter, however, are something of a kind of labor aristocracy inasmuch as they earn roughly twice the average wage of the metropolitan region and have little in common with street vendors, artisans, and household servants. Most of the urban lower classes are either mestizos who have emigrated from the countryside (or their children) and blacks, both those who are descended from West Indian laborers and those who can trace their ancestry to the colonial period. The difference between these last two is significant, since they speak different languages (English versus Spanish) and worship at different altars (Protestant versus Roman Catholic). Although there have been strenuous efforts over the years to Hispanicize the Antillean blacks, a strong U.S. presence in the zone and the pervasive draw of American popular culture have pulled in a contrary direction. Moreover, a knowledge of English has allowed this group privileged access to employment with the U.S. military community.

In a community shot through with so many divisions, the one focal point of consensus, cutting across both social and partisan divides, has been nationalism, directed primarily against the largely visible and dominant presence of the United States. As two students of Panama have written, "Nationalist sentiments have been catered to in varying degrees by all who have held positions of leadership or have sought popular support." And they assert, rather more boldly, that national leaders have "alternately responded to and contributed to an explosive climate of public opinion. They have carefully kept popular resentment narrowly focused on the United States presence, lest discontent turn on the Panamanian elite."[2]

The United States and Sources of Conflict

This task has not proved difficult, since the Republic of Panama was destined to have a conflictive relationship with the United States from the beginning. The treaty that authorized the United States to build the canal was negotiated on its behalf by an expatriate French entrepreneur, who did not even bother to consult with his putative countrymen.

Cession of a ten-mile-wide strip of national territory for the zone, which became U.S. territory "in perpetuity," effectively dismembered the infant republic and made a cruel joke of its claims to sovereignty. Within the zone, not merely U.S. laws prevailed, but the United States imposed its own customs, levied its own tariffs, and ran its own postal services. To go from the southern to the northern part of their country, Panamanians quite literally had to traverse foreign territory. In concrete terms, as late as the early 1970s, a Panamanian national caught speeding across the zone could be given a ticket (in English) by a policeman who was ignorant of all but the basics of Spanish (and perhaps not even those); the citizen was subsequently forced to appear before a U.S. magistrate, there to defend himself in proceedings conducted in English.

Quite apart from these symbolic indignities, Panamanians complained that they did not receive a fair share of receipts from the canal, that commissaries in the zone undercut Panamanian merchants in the territory of the republic, and that Panamanian workers in the zone were paid less than their American counterparts. These grievances and others as well were redressed in a piecemeal manner from the Hull-Alfaro treaty onward, but such modest conciliatory efforts could not be expected to assuage fully the feelings of envy and resentment provoked by the physical presence of a privileged American community situated at the nation's heart.

Much has been written about the zone and its inhabitants (zonians), little of it favorable. The zone itself was a monument to the capacity of Americans to replicate their society in a tropical Latin environment. The public buildings, particularly the headquarters of the Canal Company, were rendered in an architectural style unique in the world— Spanish colonial crossed with Stanford White. Not just the buildings but the broad avenues, the ceremonial open spaces, even the lampposts, struck a note of imperial self-confidence that seems incalculably remote today. It was an appropriate setting for an expatriate community of Canal Company employees defined by an unusually pugnacious variety of American nationalism, a sentiment intensified by distance and further sharpened by the uninspiring counterexample that lay just across the chain-link fences.

Though ordinary Panamanians tended to regard the zone as a kind of forbidden paradise, in reality it resembled nothing so much as a military base somewhere in the continental United States. The installations were perhaps more attractive, but there was the same sense of architectural uniformity and artificial tranquility—a town miraculously free of billboards, trash, and random commercial development. To the American eye, most of the housing developments would seem rather modest, the rough equivalent of a lower-middle-class suburb somewhere in the American South—though perhaps slightly more attractive in appearance because the dwellings themselves sat on larger lots and were painted more often. Equally impressive was the meticulous fashion in which the lawns were maintained and tropical vegetation kept at bay. It was precisely the symmetry, the coherence, the high level of maintenance of the zone that provided the starkest contrast with the territory of the republic, where, except in the most elegant neighborhoods of the rich, nothing was ever painted twice and urban planning was (and indeed remains) largely nonexistent.[3]

Inasmuch as it demonstrated what could be done with their national territory in the hands of another sovereignty, the zone constituted a kind of open wound to Panamanian self-esteem. The presence of a large U.S. military garrison also added fuel to the flame: its enlisted men were typically drawn from rural or working-class environments in the United States; most had never been abroad; few ever bothered to learn more than a few words of Spanish. Fights between drunken soldiers and Panamanian men, often over women, provided the domestic press and the political class with plenty of material to keep nationalist sentiment at fever pitch. As for the zonians, their exaggerated American patriotism often contrasted with the fact that many of their families had been resident in the area for two or three generations, and not a few of these maintained rather tenuous connections with their own country. Inevitably, they wore an air of undisguised superiority that has been the badge of every colonial administrative class in history.[4]

The United States and Sources of Advantage

As with all examples of European domination of the non-Western world, in Panama the humiliation of national sensibilities was counterbalanced by concrete benefits to broad sections of the population. U.S. technology, ingenuity, and financing bequeathed the country a physical infrastructure far superior to that of its Central American neighbors. Lake Gatún, created as an adjunct to the canal, provided Panama City with a supply of safe drinking water when such an amenity was virtually unknown in the region. Panama was also the recipient of a state-of-the-art road network and an electrical system far in advance of its own resources. U.S. health officials were vigorous in stamping out malaria, yellow fever, and other tropical diseases. From the 1960s on, U.S. Army engineering units regularly went out into the Panamanian country-side to build roads and bridges, both for training purposes and as a public relations exercise. Significantly, these operations were often carried out in areas neglected from time immemorial by authorities in the capital.

From the beginning, the U.S. dollar was used as the means of exchange in Panama. While this arguably prevented the republic from developing its own monetary policy, this method kept inflation low and simplified the country's acquisitions abroad. Significantly, no Panama-nian, even the most incendiary nationalist, has ever suggested replac-ing it with a national denomination.[5] Although Panamanians perenni-ally complained about the modest size of the annuity paid by the United States for use of the canal, they conveniently overlooked the fact that a huge U.S. military presence was translated into massive purchases of Panamanian goods and services. The amount varied over the years, but in recent times has never been less than $250 million a year and by some estimates may have reached double that amount.

Moreover, since World War II, Panama has been one of the princi-pal recipients of U.S. loans and grants in aid; between 1946 and 1996, it received $1,153,100 in various forms of assistance. Even if discount-ing the largest single transfer—$397 million in 1990, presumably to compensate for the economic embargo against General Noriega and the damages incurred during the subsequent U.S. invasion—Panama remains, at least on a per capita basis, one of the most favored of Washington's Latin American clients.[6] Among other things, American funds financed universities in Davis, Santiago de Veraguas, and Colón and a highway from Panama to El Real in the Darien peninsula.

The American presence provided another, "invisible" transfer: many millions of dollars' worth of investments were plowed into the country by foreigners, reassured by the perception that the United States would always be present—and in force—as a permanent guarantor against the vagaries of political instability. With the imminent depar-ture of the American military, Panamanians only now are beginning to worry about the loss of what for so long they took for granted.

The widespread use of English in the canal facilities and within the zone inevitably spilled out into Panama City, Colón, and other ur-ban areas. The effect was to provide Panama with a bilingual work force, the largest in Latin America, a particularly important asset in the present international business environment. The ubiquitous use of

English by Panamanians inevitably fostered closer relations between the two countries, so that probably no Latin America nation can boast so many people who genuinely understand the United States and the American mentality. In addition, American missionary communities and American civic organizations (as well as the Fulbright Scholar Program of the U.S. government) have enabled countless nonelite Panamanians to study in the United States. Because many American soldiers have married Panamanian women, some middle-class or even lower-class Panamanians have relatives in the United States. There are even a fair number of binational families among zonians.

Finally, the degree to which the two communities were separated by the barrier of language, sovereignty, and self-perception can be exaggerated. Many U.S. military people chose to rent housing in the territory of the republic. There was a fair degree of socializing between field- and senior-grade officers and English-speaking Panamanians, particularly members of the elite, as well as between Americans who did business in Panama and their local counterparts. Panamanian stores, theaters, restaurants, hotels, and recreational facilities were regularly patronized by American soldiers and their dependents, particularly on weekends; indeed, thousands of Panamanian business enterprises would not have existed without them.[7]

The Paradox of Panamanian Nationalism

U.S.-Panamanian relations have been driven over the years by an unusually intense version of the love-hate syndrome historically widespread throughout Latin America. In one way, however, the Panamanian case has been somewhat sui generis. A useful contrast is Mexico, another border country with the United States. There, anti-U.S. nationalism has been fueled by relatively abstract issues such as the historic loss of territory, discriminatory treatment of nationals in the United States, and unfavorable interest rates or import restrictions. But in Panama the bone of contention was physically present for all to see, a monument to the country's powerlessness and incapacity to take charge of its own destiny.

Small wonder that the struggle for return of the canal and the zone was, to paraphrase Sir Lewis Namier, more martyrology than history. No patriotic holiday or political demonstration failed to include pilgrimages to the tombs of the fallen—in this case, students and other agitators who over the years had perished at the hands of the police in demonstrations against the United States and the canal administration.[8] Traditionally, Panamanian political discourse has been notable for its tendency to luxuriate in victimhood and self-pity and to pose mutually exclusive demands to the United States. But, in the end, every petition was organized around a single ultimate objective: surrender of the canal and return of the zone to Panama. That for nearly three-quarters of a century no American administration would seriously contemplate either, meant that Panamanian history, thus comprehended, need never "end," since the nationalist dream would presumably never be consummated.

At the time of the ratification of the canal treaties, it is probable—though admittedly unprovable—that most Panamanians did not believe in their heart of hearts that the United States would ultimately depart. Even though the zone was immediately turned over to Panama and the transition process in canal management contemplated in the treaties began immediately and adhered rigorously to its schedule, throughout the 1980s the Panamanian press and Panamanian political life were full of allegations that the United States was cheating on its obligations or planning to wiggle out of them somehow in the end. This discourse became more strident in the late 1980s, when the Reagan and Bush administrations began their efforts to oust strongman General Manuel Noriega, commander in chief of the Panamanian Defense Forces (FDP). Indeed, the American invasion of 1989 was widely interpreted as a sign that the United States was planning to take back everything conceded in Carter-Torrijos. When this proved untrue, the country entered an acute crisis of identity from which it has yet to emerge. In effect, the principal victim of the canal treaties and the surrender of the zone has been Panamanian nationalism itself.

Panamanian Opinion Today

To the extent that Panamanians realize that the United States is indeed leaving, they have turned inward to reflect on the quality of their own institutions and leadership. What they find does not provide much comfort to Panama's political class. Perhaps for the first time, people in public life have begun to express doubts about their country that they would have kept locked inside themselves as recently as ten years earlier. One example is a 1996 television interview with Foreign Minister Ricardo Roberto Arias. The reporter suddenly asked, "Why should the rest of the nations believe" us, "who at this time do not seem to be very good at handling ourselves internally (since we are always squabbling and having problems).... How are we going to tell the rest of the world, 'Look, we are currently not able to, but we will manage the Canal.'" The best response the normally smooth, self-satisfied foreign minister could manage was, "Panama has to rise above its internal conflicts and understand that the benefits that we may draw from [the Canal], which is what ultimately counts, lie in the seriousness and restraint with which we handle that entity step by step."

"But this is a radical change," the interviewer persisted, "because we remain the same Panamanians, with the same happy-go-lucky tropical sentiment, or as someone once said, with somewhat of a Caribbean sense of life." Then, pressing further, he asked, "How are we going to succeed with a little sentiment or national pride in rising over what is happening? I find, and you will pardon me, a sentiment of frustration among Panamanians."[9]

The chief beneficiary of this change of mood has been, correspondingly, the United States. Three recent polls make this clear. The first survey was conducted in June 1992, shortly before a visit by President George Bush, and casts perhaps surprising light on the way that Panamanians have come to view bilateral issues. Some 80 percent of the respondents expressed a desire for "some" U.S. troop presence in the country after the year 2000, with fully 46 percent favoring the maintenance of 1992 levels. Thirty-six percent even asserted that U.S. troops should be primarily responsible for dealing with any attempted coup against a constitutional government in Panama, "using force if necessary." Most thought that the government was not sufficiently prepared to take control of the canal and questioned the current utilization of its income. Hence, it cannot be surprising that two-thirds of those questioned thought that the canal should be jointly administered by Panama and the United States. More striking, *only one-fifth of the respondents favored exclusive Panamanian control.*

The second poll, carried out in 1993 and funded by the U.S. National Democratic Institute of International Affairs, was based on fourteen focus groups throughout the republic. In putting this survey together, great care was taken to combine rural and urban, suburban and small town, as well as diverse educational and economic backgrounds.[10] The poll found a sense of overwhelming "disappointment and resentment" in the country, largely driven by a growing distrust in government, politicians, and political parties, whom those interviewed regarded as "disconnected" from the people. Many told pollsters that conditions had worsened since the return of democracy (that is, the ouster of Noriega and the installation of an elected president, Manuel Endara).

When asked about their perception of the nation's biggest problem, about half mentioned unemployment (respondents repeatedly claimed that jobs were harder to find now than during military regimes). One-quarter mentioned crime and drug trafficking. The latter was alleged to be worse even than under the Noriega regime, apparently because of the lack of effective public order. This response underscores the low degree of confidence inspired by the Public Force, the police formation created by the Endara government with U.S. cooperation to replace the FDP after the invasion. (A twenty-six-year-old gasoline station employee in Panama City said: "Now they'll kill you in the street to steal a pair of pants and no one will help. The police are too afraid. Before, the police was there to be help us.") The third vice most often mentioned was corruption. This was defined as misappropriation of government monies, as well as the widespread use of Mafia tactics to keep power and jobs within the political families of the oligarchy. (One taxi driver, forty-four, in Panama City, remarked that "before we had a dictatorship of the military, now we have a dictatorship of the oligarchy.")

The constant reference to the oligarchy suggests a nostalgia, if not for populist military governments as such, then for the extinguished caudillo Omar Torrijos. The focus groups were by no means uncritical of Torrijos' s rule and freely admitted its deficiencies, but, they insisted, at least he thought about the country "from the bottom up." Respondents credited Torrijos for keeping his promises—to deliver roads, schools, and so forth—in contrast to the present government. Not much faith, however, was placed in the opposition, which the respondents basically regarded as a group of self-seeking politicians interested only in their own advancement. The report goes on, "Voters believe that the political parties have a clear and discernible message, but that their messages are essentially all the same. (If you vote for us, everything will be better …) and that as soon as they're elected they will forget everything they promised in the campaign."

Significantly, of all the political parties, only Torrijos's (and Noriega's) Democratic Revolutionary Party was seen as different, with a sense that it at least stood for something. Generally speaking, those Panamanians surveyed thought that Panama had too many political parties anyway—two or three would be quite enough, instead of the half-dozen or more. They would be happy with fewer promises and more action. ("Be honest with us, and get busy moving the country forward.")

The third poll, commissioned by the U.S. Information Agency from the local CID-Gallup affiliate in January 1996, underscores the degree to which the United States can no longer serve as a useful whipping boy for Panamanian politicians.[11] According to this survey, eight of ten Panamanians harbor a favorable view of this country, a rating among the highest anywhere in the Western Hemisphere. Good opinion is generally consistent across all demographic groups, though it is somewhat more favorable outside Panama City than within it and almost twice as high among the least educated sectors compared with the best educated. This is all the more remarkable considering that this poll was conducted almost six years after the U.S. invasion, which occasioned some loss of life and considerable loss of property, largely in the poorer areas of the capital. During this same period, the U.S. Congress failed to fund fully President George Bush's request for a $1 billion aid package for the country. And, what is more, talks with the United States over a possible residual base presence after the year 2000 had recently broken down when it became clear that Washington did not intend to offer Panama financial compensation in exchange.

On no subject have Panamanians been more frequently polled since 1990 than on their views of a permanent U.S. military presence after the year 2000. In twenty-nine surveys reported in the Panamanian press since March 1991, not a single one decisively rejects the idea, and most favor it, in many cases by majorities as high as 76 percent. The only variable is the introduction of the issue of base rents. As late as 1995, a significant plurality continued to favor U.S. retention of at least some of its military properties even in the absence of a compensation package,[12] although opinion on that score has gradually turned around since 1996 (see chapter 5).

One particular survey[13] deserves to be explored in detail for the light it sheds on the texture of Panamanian opinion. It began by affirming that 75.6 percent favored U.S. bases in Panama after the year 2000. Of those who said yes, the reasons given were

Income (through salaries, purchases, etc.) 25.9%
Security 13.4%
They run the canal better 7.4%
Will create more jobs 6.5%
Panama will be safer 3.6%
Don't know/no answer 1.5%

The minority (24.4 percent) opposing a permanent U.S. military presence expressed the reasons, however deeply felt, in somewhat abstract terms: the struggle for sovereignty, "it all belongs to Panama," "they were invaders," the need for independence. Conversely, those who favored U.S. bases were concrete in their expectations. Some 71.3 percent doubted that Panama "will have the capability to absorb the Panamanians left jobless" when the Americans leave; 68.5 percent thought that the current U.S. military presence actually helped to "guarantee political stability and democracy in Panama"; and 61.7 percent doubted that such a presence would contribute to the militarization of the Panamanian police. When asked whether the gradual transition from the 1950s to the 1970s of the National Police to National Guard (and, later, to the Panamanian Defense Forces) was significantly influenced by the U.S. military presence, 47.7 percent thought that it had "no influence," while 41.8 percent agreed that it had played a role. (Almost 11 percent had no opinion or did not answer the question.)

When the same question was posed even more acutely, namely, whether "the Panamanian military dictatorship was highly influenced, somewhat influenced, or not influenced at all by the presence of the U.S. military in our country," 49.6 percent responded "great" or "some" influence, but 50.4 percent said "little" or "no" influence. The response to both questions shows that, whatever the facts of the case, ordinary Panamanians tend to "remember" their recent past rather differently from many of their historians or public figures or, for that matter, many American journalists.

The questions that touch on Panamanian attitudes toward the United States and Americans in general, including Americans resident in Panama, are even more interesting to the extent that they raise serious questions about the degree to which Yankeephobia, so striking a feature of Panamanian politics in the past, has either disappeared almost completely or never existed to the degree imagined by the U.S. negotiators of the canal treaties, U.S. politicians and journalists, and the American public.

QUESTION. In general, how would you rate your liking for the United States and North Americans?

Do like..69.4%
Do not like..18.4%
Don't know/no answer.................................12.1%

QUESTION. How do you feel when you see U.S. soldiers on the streets in Panama?

Indifferent 44.5%
"Makes you feel good" 42.6%
"Makes you feel bad" 12.9%

QUESTION. Do you think that the presence of U.S. bases in Panama enhances or tarnishes our image before other countries in the world?

Favors 61.9%
"Tarnishes" 24.7%
Don't know/no answer 13.4%

QUESTION. How do you feel that the U.S. presence has affected Panamanian customs and lifestyle since the construction of the canal?

Has enriched them 40.0%
Has yielded a few benefits 27.4%
Has caused a little damage 12.7%
Has caused great damage 12.4%
Don't know/no answer 7.5%

The favorable opinion of the United States and its citizens held by ordinary Panamanians may well be simply the logical and inevitable fruit of the Carter-Torrijos treaties, which removed, however gradually, the bone of contention between the two countries. Alternatively, Panamanian nationalist sentiment or Panamanian Yankeephobia may have been far more superficial a phenomenon than either seemed at the time. Whatever the case, over the past ten or fifteen years, terms of the U.S.-Panamanian equation have been utterly transformed. The willingness of the United States to give a small country what it wanted has finally eliminated a historic grievance, but—and here is the paradox—it has radically altered its political landscape, to such an extent indeed that the small country has been tempted to dismiss its earlier claims as being of little or no significance ("We didn't really mean it."). The matter has been put succinctly by Christian Democratic leader Milton Henríquez: "Now that the divorce is coming, we are in a state of denial."[14] Given that both countries have already proceeded far down the path laid out by Carter-Torrijos, this collective state of mind poses serious problems for those who must govern Panama after the year 2000.

Panamanian Politics from the Protectorate
to Torrijos, 1903–1968

Understanding just what those problems might be requires a brief overview of Panamanian political history. From its separation from Colombia in 1903 to the late 1930s, the country was basically a U.S. protectorate, in the sense that it could hardly be regarded as genuinely independent. It did not even possess an army of its own, since an abortive military conspiracy in 1904 led the Americans to disband Panama's infant armed forces and replace them with a national police. The Hay–Bunau Varilla treaty had established residual guardianship rights for the United States, including the right to intervene in the country's internal affairs. In many ways, the situation resembled the U.S. relationship with Cuba under the Platt amendment, though the United States exercised its authority with far greater abandon in Panama. The treaties, for example, supposedly limited the deployment of U.S. troops to protection of the canal. This right was not taken to prohibit the stationing of American troops to protect U.S. citizens and property in the northern province of Chiriquí for two years, even though the area, which borders on Costa Rica, was nowhere near the canal installations. Moreover, U.S. diplomatic personnel served throughout this period as advisers to Panamanian officials, and U.S. functionaries supervised Panamanian elections, though admittedly at the request of incumbent governments.

By 1920, the United States had intervened directly into Panama's political life four times, all but once at the request of contending political factions. Indeed, as in Cuba during the same period, the name of the game for the losing side in any contest was to coax the United States into tilting the balance back in its favor. Meanwhile, the U.S. garrison was occasionally employed as a force of last resort when the domestic tranquility was threatened by political upheaval. When a popular protest against an increase in housing rents proved more than the Panamanian government could handle in 1925, the United States provided it with 600 troops, who with fixed bayonets dispersed crowds that might otherwise have seized the capital. When the United States declined to interfere with a palace coup in 1931—the first such successful adventure in Panamanian political history—something of a watershed was reached.

During the early years of the republic, political life was dominated by a handful of elite families. Thus, any political competition took place between people who knew one another and in many cases were related. That pattern was broken for the first time in 1932, when Harmodio Arias Madrid was elected to the presidency. A mestizo from a poor provincial family, Arias was a graduate of the London School of Economics and the author of a book denouncing the Monroe Doctrine. He was the quintessential representative of Panama's emerging urban middle class, committed to populist economic policies and driven by resentment of the United States. Arias was also the first president to show any serious interest in delivering government services to the long-neglected countryside. He established the University of Panama, which became a hothouse of nationalist sentiment and an enduring source of political unrest. Perhaps Arias's most notable achievement was coaxing the United States into revising Hay–Bunau Varilla; in the Hull-Alfaro accords (1936) Washington renounced the right of unilateral intervention, a measure roughly congruent with President Franklin D. Roosevelt's unilateral abrogation of the Platt amendment two years earlier.

The more sinister face of Panamanian populism was revealed in 1940 with the election of Arias's brother, Arnulfo, to the presidency as the candidate of the new Panameñista Party. An accomplished demagogue capable of unleashing mob violence with a flick of his wrist, Arnulfo Arias cast himself as the scourge of American imperialism and also of Panama's numerous non-Hispanic minorities, whom he proposed to deport at the first opportunity. Arias's purported admiration for the triumphant Axis in Europe, as well as the suspicion that he was in touch with Nazi and Fascist agents, provoked genuine concern, as did his efforts to rewrite the constitution to extend his presidential term. His ouster by the National Police while out of the country in October 1941 was greeted with undisguised relief by both Washington and the Panamanian establishment.

Nonetheless, Arias's political career was notable for its extraordinary longevity. Before his death in 1988, he was elected three more times (possibly five more if his followers' claims concerning the elections of 1964 and 1984 are to be taken seriously), though he was never allowed to serve a full term. Even so, Arias set much of the tone for Panamanian political life from the fifth to the seventh decades of the present century and indeed beyond them: even in death, he continues to command the multitudes, since his widow, Mireya Moscoso, a woman of great personal charm but limited political talent, came within a hairbreadth of winning the presidency in 1994.

The role of the National Police in Arias's ouster is wholly emblematic, for during the 1940s and 1950s it emerged, together with the oligarchy and Arnulfo Arias, as the third wheel of Panamanian politics. Here the key figure was José Antonio Remón, who during the period 1948–1952 was the power behind the throne, installing, ousting, and reinstalling presidents. Most of his time, however, was spent transforming the National Police into a paramilitary force, improving their salaries and equipment, and strengthening his relations with U.S. military authorities. Remón was elected to the presidency in 1952 as the candidate of the National Patriotic Coalition; the following year he reorganized the National Police as the National Guard, thus restoring to Panama the army it had lost a half-century before.

In some ways, Remón was a precursor of General Torrijos, at least to the extent that he tried to build a popular base of his own through modest social reforms and the diversification of Panama's narrow economic base. His agricultural and industrial programs did temporarily decrease the country's overwhelming dependence on the canal and the zone, but, like other experiments in import substitution elsewhere in Latin America, their weakness would have been revealed over time. (In the event, they were dismantled by his successor.) Remón quite possibly was inspired to some degree by Argentina's General Juan Perón, as were a number of other Latin American military presidents in those years. Remón did not live to complete his term: he was assassinated at the Panama City racetrack in 1955 under mysterious circumstances—here again, a parallel with Torrijos—possibly at the behest of the U.S. Mafia.

The four presidents who followed Remón—Ricardo Arias (1955–1956), Ricardo de la Guardia (1956–1960), Roberto Chiari (1960–1964), and Marco Robles (1964–1968)—were all drawn from the oligarchy and, as such, were forced to rely heavily on the National Guard in the face of increasing challenges from Arnulfo Arias's followers, as well as random explosions of street violence, typically to protest some aspect of continued U.S. control of the canal and the zone. Gamal Abdel Nasser's seizure of the Suez Canal facility was an obvious goad, as was the flying of the Panamanian flag inside the zone in 1964 (described in chapter 2). In looking back on these years, what strikes the observer is the degree to which Panamanian politics had reached something of a stalemate. Despite its multitude of parties and slogans, as well as the general sophistication of its urban centers, the content of public life remained remarkably thin. The only parties with clearly identifiable programs, the Christian Democrats and the Socialists, were extremely small, whereas Arnulfo Arias's Panameñistas, who had a genuine mass following, had no known agenda, apart from their desire to see the Americans depart as soon as possible, and certainly nothing that could be called an ideology. This system was brought down by a coup in 1968.

The Torrijos Years, 1968–1981

The proximate cause of this 1968 coup was a hotly disputed presidential election in which the victor was Arnulfo Arias. Taking office for the last time on October 1, Arias announced his intention to purge the leadership of the National Guard and replace its commanders with officers of his own choosing. The resulting barracks revolt sent the new president and his entire cabinet scuttling into the Canal Zone for their own physical protection and from there into exile. The National Assembly and all political parties were dissolved, and the University of Panama was closed for several months while its faculty and student body were vetted for subversive activities or opinions. There was strong popular resistance to the coup, not merely students and workers, but inhabitants of the slum areas of Panama City and even peasants in the distant provinces of Chiriquí and Bocas del Toro. Nonetheless, after several turbulent months, the guard emerged fully in control of the situation.

The ruling junta was originally led by Colonel José María Panilla. Within a matter of months, he was replaced as provisional president by Demetrio Lakas, an engineer with good connections to Panama's business establishment. As time went on, the rhetoric and, to some degree, the policies of the government veered leftward, with a plethora of tax, land, labor, educational, and agrarian reforms that borrowed freely from military socialist regimes of the day in Bolivia and Peru and also (in educational areas) from Fidel Castro's Cuba. These developments are directly related to the rise of General Omar Torrijos, commander of the National Guard, who in 1972 was proclaimed head of the government and "maximum leader of the Panamanian Revolution."

Omar Torrijos was undoubtedly one of the most colorful figures ever to walk the Panamanian political stage. A swashbuckling officer risen from relatively humble origins, he had a rough-and-ready charm and a capacity for improvisation that delighted his followers and confounded his opponents. Torrijos owed his rapid ascent in the first instance to his mastery of the intricacies of Panamanian military politics.

But his enduring power rested on a capacity to build a political base that was both broad and deep, melding together formerly antagonistic political forces: students and soldiers, peasants and urban workers, middle-class bureaucrats and high-flying bankers.

In the art of wrapping himself in the Panamanian flag, Torrijos far outdid Arnulfo Arias; unlike the hapless Arias, he had the good fortune to preside over his country's fortunes when the United States was becoming increasingly disposed to negotiate its withdrawal from the canal and the zone. In so doing, it provided Torrijos with much of the glue that held his coalition together. Time was also on the caudillo's side: new and more liberal banking laws, enacted on the eve of the first oil shock of 1971, positioned Panama to siphon off resources from the massive recycling of petrodollars. The same global upsurge in liquidity allowed Panama, like other Latin American countries, to borrow heavily to finance housing projects, public works, and the acquisition of sophisticated military hardware, as well as to provide much middle-class employment through an expanded bureaucracy. Torrijos revamped Panama's educational system to stress vocational skills over the liberal arts, and he built schools and clinics in the remotest areas of the interior, the first time such services had ever been extended by any Panamanian government so far from the country's urban core. By the end of Torrijos's presidency, however, the country labored under the heaviest debt burden per capita in the world.

For a brief period—roughly 1971–1973—Torrijos had something to offer nearly everybody. After that, his Panamanian revolution was forced into something of a *Thermidor* by inflation, as well as by excessively generous social legislation, which could not be supported by the country's levels of production. Thanks to authoritarian security laws, the absence of organized political parties, and a captive media—as well as the timely jailing or forcible expatriation of potential rivals or troublemakers combined with Torrijos's capacity to hijack the canal issue—the government faced no immediate challenge. Once ratified, however, the canal treaties deprived Torrijos of protective coloration, since his opponents no longer felt obliged to keep their silence. Moreover, the Carter administration, which had shamefacedly tried to evade questions about the true nature of the Torrijos regime at the Senate hearings,[15] privately exacted from him a promise to retire from politics after ratification. Consequently, security laws were relaxed or repealed, exiles permitted to return, and opposition parties were permitted to reorganize. There were limits, however, to Torrijos's willingness to relinquish power. An official Democratic Revolutionary Party (PRD) was created to perpetuate his legacy, and in October 1978 a puppet National Assembly elected the PRD's handpicked candidate, Aristides Royo, to a six-year presidential term. Torrijos resumed his former title as commander of the National Guard.

Torrijos's Coalition Falls Apart, 1981–1990

Most Panamanians regarded Royo, a young lawyer and former minister of education, as a nonentity who was merely keeping the presidential seat warm until Torrijos could run for president in 1984. Torrijos's unexpected demise in a freak plane accident in 1981 threw Panama into a full-blown succession crisis. Royo, who quarreled with the National Guard leadership, was quickly replaced the following year by his vice-president, Ricardo de la Espriella, who in turn was replaced in 1984 (through fraudulent elections) by Nicolás Ardito Barletta, a former vice-president of the World Bank with no power base of his own. With the disappearance of Torrijos, power in Panama was increasingly centered in the National Guard (after 1983, the Panamanian Defense Forces—FDP), whose dominant personality was its chief of intelligence (subsequently its commander), General Manuel Noriega.

Noriega had all of Torrijos's vices and none of his virtues. Unpopular from the start, he chose to rule indirectly through a series of civilian puppets. This system proved more difficult than expected, since the weight of Noriega's demands taxed the loyalty of the most craven accomplices. Barletta was forced to resign after less than a year in office, partly because Noriega feared—perhaps groundlessly—that he would succumb to pressures both from the U.S. Congress and from within Panama to investigate the murder of Dr. Hugo Spadafora. (Spadafora was a government critic who claimed to have hard evidence of Noriega's involvement in drug trafficking.) His replacement, Vice-President Eric Arturo Delvalle, though even more subservient than his predecessor, nonetheless failed to satisfy the Panamanian strongman. Impeached by Noriega's handpicked legislature, he was replaced by Education Minister Manuel Solís Palma. Unfortunately for Noriega, the United States insisted on continuing to recognize Delvalle's government, although for the next five years its only point of contact with it was the Panamanian embassy in Washington and the U.S. embassy residence in Panama City, where the putative president languished in semicaptivity as the house guest of Ambassador Arthur Davis.[16]

These splits within Torrijos's old coalition opened new opportunities for the opposition. A National Civic Crusade (CCN), led by civic and business leaders, but comprehending most of Panama's pre-Torrijos political parties, organized anti-Noriega marches and demonstrations. FDP troops responded harshly and closed down the independent media outlets that had been permitted to reopen during Torrijos's final years. Elections were scheduled for May 7, 1989, and opposition activities began to focus on organizing an effective anti-Noriega coalition. The opposition ticket, led by Guillermo Endara of the new Arnulfista party (named after the recently expired Arias), also included Ricardo Arias Calderón of the Christian Democrats (PDC) and Guillermo Ford of the National Liberal Republican Movement (MOLIRENA) as first and second vice-presidents, respectively. The opposition won the election by a three-to-one majority, but Solís Palma's government refused to recognize the results, even though they were confirmed by an international observer delegation led by former U.S. President Jimmy Carter. Indeed, Noriega's goons set on and brutally beat up supporters of the victorious candidates, expelled foreign journalists who had reported this and other atrocities,[17] and accelerated the systematic harassment of U.S. military and diplomatic personnel, which had begun shortly after Noriega's indictment.

The gradual estrangement between Panama's military leaders and the United States was not without its ironic aspects. Although Torrijos had supported the Nicaraguan Sandinistas before their seizure of power, by early 1981 he was coming to view them (and also the FMLN guerrilla movement in El Salvador) through much the same ideological lens as the new administration of President Ronald Reagan. The warming of relations between Panama City and Washington was all the more unexpected given the fact that Reagan occupied a special place in the demonology of the PRD. (He had made his political career by opposing the canal treaties in the 1976 Republican presidential primaries.)

Torrijos's death in no way diminished the new cordiality, which probably reached its highest point around 1984. Although sophisticated members of the U.S. intelligence community had few illusions about Noriega, who was visibly moving to consolidate his position as Torrijos's successor, they were happy to have him on board. (They often joked that even if he was playing a double game, selling his services simultaneously to Cuba and the United States, it was good to have him in the U.S. camp at least 50 percent of the time.)[18] Moreover, as head of the FDP (after 1983), Noriega commanded what was after the year 2000 to be the sole military force to protect and defend the canal, which—like it or not—recommended close relations with him and his colleagues.[19]

The U.S.-Noriega confrontation was the product of events both deliberate and accidental. From the mid-1980s onward, there was a tactical convergence in the U.S. Congress between conservative Republicans and liberal Democrats; the former, many of whom had opposed the canal treaties a decade before, seized on the growing political disorder in Panama to discredit the notion of devolution; the latter, now liberated from the need to cover for Torrijos (and Carter), suddenly discovered that Panama had a human rights problem. In June 1987, the Senate passed a resolution calling for a transition to genuine democracy in Panama. When Noriega's people organized demonstrations against the U.S. embassy and arrested diplomatic personnel, Washington cut off all military and economic assistance. At the end of the year, Congress suspended Panama's share of the sugar quota, terminated all nonhumanitarian aid, prohibited joint military exercises, and mandated U.S. opposition to multilateral loans until Noriega handed over the reins of power to an elected civilian government.

Events took an unexpected turn in February 1988, when grand juries in Miami and Tampa indicted Noriega on various counts of racketeering, drug trafficking, and money laundering, which made it impossible for any administration, with the best will in the world, to contemplate doing business with him. (For their part, Noriega and his supporters steadfastly refused to believe that the judicial system in the United States operated independently of the executive and regarded the finding as a deliberate provocation organized from the White House.) When Delvalle was forced out of office the same month, the United States froze $50 million in Panamanian assets in the United States, withheld its monthly payment for canal use (which was put into escrow for Delvalle's government), and suspended Panama's access to the Generalized System of Trade Preferences (GSP).

As relations deteriorated, Noriega was increasingly emboldened to bait the United States, which he was apparently certain would never use force to depose him, least of all under President George Bush, whom he regarded as weak and ineffectual. The misconception may well have drawn sustenance from the fact that, to the end, U.S. authorities were secretly trying to convince Noriega to resign quietly and agree to plea bargain the charges pending against him. The crisis was brought to a head by Article 3, section 3[c], of the canal treaties, which required the president of the United States to nominate (together with the government of Panama) a new canal administrator of Panamanian nationality to take office on January 1, 1990. Clearly, this could not be accomplished with a puppet regime that Washington did not even recognize. This issue, together with the threat of escalating mob violence against U.S. nationals by Noriega's "Dignity Battalions," led President Bush to order an invasion force of 12,000 troops into the country on December 20, 1989.[20] President Endara and his cabinet were sworn into office on a U.S. military base, and Noriega captured and taken to the United States for confinement and eventual trial. Although many predicted that Noriega's troops would fight to the finish, exacting a high human cost from the United States, battles were few and brief; most casualties resulted from fires ignited by the U.S. forces and also by the Dignity Battalions to cover their escape.[21] The most important consequence of the U.S. invasion was not, however, the overthrow of Noriega's regime, but the demobilization of the FDP and its gradual replacement by something called the Public Force (FP), a police force somewhat similar to what the country had possessed until the early 1950s.

Since Noriega, 1990–

Though elected by an overwhelming majority, the Endara administration quickly squandered its accumulated political capital. The new president himself turned out to be a pleasant, somewhat mild-mannered voluptuary whose main interest appeared to be the feathering his own nest.[22] His personal popularity, which was at the eightieth percentile at the beginning of his term, plunged to the single digits four years later. To some degree, this resulted from circumstances beyond his control: many Panamanians expected the U.S. invasion to resolve all their problems in one fell swoop, and the failure of the American Congress to compensate Panama adequately for invasion damages (as well as for the economic embargo slapped on the Noriega regime in its final months) inevitably redounded to Endara's discredit, to the extent to which he was seen—in many ways wrongly —as Washington's man.

The Endara years were punctuated by rumors of corruption, narcotics trafficking, petty politics, and favoritism, as well as quarrels within the government coalition. Vice-President Ricardo Arías Calderón, whose Christian Democrats were effectively excluded from power since 1991, resigned at the end of the following year. Parties continued to proliferate, assuring that whoever was elected in 1994 would not have a governing majority. Political stability was guaranteed at the beginning by the presence of a large U.S. constabulary force and, as that body was drawn down, by the absence of a praetorian guard in the form of the FDP. Conversely, one study published in 1992 cast troubling light on the long-term social situation. It found that 40 percent of Panamanians in urban areas were unemployed or underemployed (45 percent in rural areas). More than half between the ages of fifteen and twenty-four were unemployed, and two-thirds of those had even given up looking for work. Three of eight Panamanians were adjudged to live in poverty or extreme poverty. The study also established that income disparities in Panama were among the highest in Latin America.[23]

Popular expectations were therefore piled heavily onto the 1994 elections, the first since the American invasion. The PRD, having recovered somewhat from the discredit in which it had languished four years before, wisely nominated a civilian, Ernesto Pérez Balladares. A U.S.-educated banker who had served various military-dominated administrations as minister of finance and planning, as well as director of the national hydroelectric authority, Pérez Balladares was the respectable face of the PRD, the quintessential representative of its opening to Panama's business community. Although the opposition made valiant efforts to tar him with the brush of the military dictatorships he had once served, Pérez Balladares's sober demeanor and his refusal to engage in incendiary rhetoric left his opponents somewhat nonplused.

Moreover, unlike 1990, the anti-PRD forces could not forge a common front. The Christian Democrats, MOLIRENA, and the Arnulfistas each ran candidates of their own, as did Arnulfo Arias's old Panameñistas (rechristened Doctrinal Panameñistas, to distinguish themselves from the Arnulfistas, as the party's main branch was now known). To confuse matters further, salsa singer Ruben Blades, a Panamanian celebrity usually residing in Los Angeles, returned to form a party of his own, Papa Egoro (Mother Earth), which ran ahead of all others in the early polls, more as a sign of disaffection with Panama's old political class than anything else.

The campaign itself was notable for the degree to which the candidates circled around the hard issues. All promised to create more jobs, though most of their proposals were vague or unrealistic. A similar lack of clarity pervaded pronouncements on crime, infrastructure, and corruption. All the candidates except MOLIRENA's Manuel Carlés vehemently opposed a residual base presence for the United States after the year 2000, and Carlés entertained the thought only by raising the possibility of preferential trade arrangements with the United States as a form of compensation.[24] As election day approached, the best the anti-PRD forces could do was to stage a dramatic broadcast by President Endara, in which he presented a "documentary" film on the bad old days of Panama under the PRD—emphasizing crime, corruption, mismanagement, and, above all, a cynical attitude toward power and toward the Panamanian people. Although the documentary producers must have looked far and wide for footage capable of discrediting Pérez Balladares, they came up with pretty thin gruel—nothing that could compromise him directly with illicit enrichment or the mistreatment of political opponents.

The results were conclusive only to the extent that Panama's first-past-the-post system assures a victory on the first ballot. No candidate won anything like a majority, and the winner—Pérez Balladares—gained only 33.3 percent of the vote. His most formidable opponent turned out to be Arnulfo Arias's widow, Mireya Moscoso, whose Arnulfista party garnered nearly as much, 29.1 percent. (Blades and Carlés claimed 17 and 16 percent of the vote, respectively.) Señora Moscoso's showing was all the more remarkable in that, quite apart from never before running for office, she refused to take part in the two televised presidential debates. Thus, while those who voted for the PRD may conceivably have been fantasizing about a return to the good old days of free-spending (and free-borrowing) Omar Torrijos, it is difficult to know just what thousands of Arnulfista militants had in mind, except to oppose the (now extinguished) Panamanian military or anyone ever associated with it.

The Panamanian Dilemma

For many years, the basic fault lines of Panamanian politics have run not along a left-right axis, but between "formal" democracy, which more or less respected civil liberties but was basically unrepresentative of much of Panamanian society, and military (or quasi-military, or military-backed) populism, which displayed scant regard for constitutional decencies but which found broad and deep resonance among the country's have-nots. Since his election in 1994, Pérez Balladares has tried to close the gap between the two political cultures by reaching out to the *civilista* opposition and offering important positions to members of other parties. The result has been a cabinet more diverse and perhaps more qualified than Panama has ever had but, for all that, less representative than the new president might have wished, since the Arnulfistas have rigidly turned aside his offers of participation.

Meanwhile, the old guard of the PRD, including ex-officers of the demobilized FDP, have continually expressed their apprehensions about this unexpected generosity to opponents, as have the unions, slum dwellers, students, and others who are suspicious of a new and more "respectable" version of *Torrijismo*. The widening gap between Pérez Balladares and his followers is the product of wholly different worldviews. Panama's president understands that the days of boom-and-spend populism are gone, not just in Panama but everywhere in Latin America; that in an increasingly global economy Panama must become more competitive; and that new incentives are needed to replace the diminishing assets of a dwindling U.S. military presence. His followers, however, continue to draw sustenance from the anti-imperialist doctrines that they were taught by his predecessors; insofar as domestic politics are concerned, they cannot readily grasp why the past—rich in patronage, public works, and abundant rewards for loyalty to the PRD and its leaders—cannot be restored.

The persistent divergence between these two political communities is particularly troubling in light of two other facts. First, the Panamanian military no longer exists as a balance wheel between domestic political factions; second, the United States, always the court of final appeal when conflicts between Panamanians reach deadlock,[25] is preparing to withdraw from the scene. The 1989 invasion was the last episode in Panamanian history to highlight this latter role; with the departure of the United States, the country's only sure sense of political gravity will have disappeared. Indeed, beneath the rhetoric of the 1994 campaign, one could perceive an underlying note of regret that this was the case, to the point that many politicians simply refused to adjust to the new realities and continued to attack phantoms rather than confront the serious questions.

Panama's future still depends in a large measure on its crucial geographical position and its possession of one of the world's major interoceanic facilities. But it does so under a wholly new set of circumstances. The pregnant social and racial inequalities that have been long sublimated by Panamanian nationalism must now be negotiated without compromising the country's political stability, while at the same time insulating its major economic resource—the canal—from temptations that threaten to undermine its contribution to national welfare. A closer look at the facility itself is therefore in order.

4

★

The Canal

One of the engineering marvels of the world, the Panama Canal has been in continuous service since its opening in 1914. Roughly 5 percent of the world's trade passes through its locks, and more than 60 percent originates or terminates at U.S. ports (some 14 percent of total U.S. seaborne trade). Canal tolls account for some 9 percent to Panama's gross domestic product, though its contributions to the republic's welfare go far beyond this: the facility has led to a proliferation of service-oriented activities that employ thousands of people. These include storage, ship repair, break bulk (the unloading of part or all of a ship's cargo), transshipment, bunkering, and the provisioning and hosteling of ship travelers.

American army engineers and labor forces drawn from many countries succeeded in building a path between the seas by damming up the Chagrés River, which created a huge artificial lake (Gatún) in the middle of the isthmus (see map, frontispiece). Enormous ditches, or rather channels, were then excavated to each coast, and locks were built to raise and lower the ships between sea level and Lake Gatún. In effect, three sets of locks were built: the Gatún locks on the Atlantic side and the Pedro Miguel and Miraflores locks on the Pacific side. The lock chambers themselves are approximately 303 meters long by 33 meters wide; these measurements limit vessel size to approximately 287 meters in length and 32 meters in width. These dimensions are somewhat outdated in terms of contemporary ship construction, insofar as the canal cannot be transited by either oil supertankers or many of the newer bulk cargo carriers. This situation, among other things, has led to the creation of a joint Panamanian-Japanese-U.S. commission to study means of widening the passage. This problem is far from academic, since half the fifteen hours of transiting the canal is consumed by waiting for access.

While ordinary Panamanians have long regarded the canal as a kind of milch cow that, once recovered for the national patrimony, would assure every citizen an effortless and prosperous existence—somewhat similar to the role oil plays in Kuwait—for all its engineering sophistication the facility is old and requires constant maintenance, roughly a quarter of its $400 million annual budget. Far from being a major source of revenues, it barely breaks even. It cannot be run at a loss, with inflated payrolls and noncompetitive acquisition of goods and services, as is the case with so many other public enterprises in Panama. The dichotomy between popular expectations and hard economic facts has been steadily revealed to public view since at least 1990, when a Panamanian administrator took charge of the facility.

Canal Operation—Issues, Problems, and Predictions

Tolls and Traffic. Immediately before the ratification hearings in 1977–1978, the Department of State and the Panama Canal Company commissioned a study to project traffic and revenues. When the author of this study, economist Ely M. Brandes, was invited to present his findings to the Senate Foreign Relations Committee, he cautioned that the calculus between toll increases and actual revenue was exceedingly narrow. Starting at the level of 15–20 percent increases, traffic would drop off; while the return per ship would increase as the charges grew, even at the rate of a 50 percent increase in tolls the loss of customers would nearly neutralize the economic benefit.

"The very maximum amount of revenue," he told the senators, "that could be obtained was only about 40 percent more than the revenue that was projected without any toll increases. To get this maximum amount we would require an increase of somewhere between 75 and 100 percent." Raising tolls was severely limited because "many, if not most, users of the canal" had other cheaper—or not more expensive—alternatives available to them.[1]

These alternatives, Brandes explained, depended on the product being shipped and its unit value, as well as the kinds of carriers available. Dry bulk material, such as coal dispatched from the eastern United States to Japanese markets, could be competitively transported in bulk carriers of about 100,000 deadweight tons around the Cape of Good Hope. Television sets from Japan, secured in containers, could be unloaded at Los Angeles or Seattle, and from there shipped by rail to the U.S. East Coast. Lumber from British Columbia to the eastern United States could be profitably moved across the North American continent by rail. Oil or petroleum products, such as jet fuel, could be exchanged rather than shipped by cooperating producers and customers in different parts of the world. Or, if canal tolls became too oppressive, markets could rearrange themselves. Brandes cited the case of iron ore from Peru. Instead of sending it through Panama, Peru could ship directly via the Pacific to Japan, and the United States could rely more heavily on domestic sources. Brandes told the committee that

> with respect to all of these alternatives, the buyers and sellers involved appear to be almost equally well-off whether they use the Canal or choose an alternative. The fact that the shift to alternatives can occur as a consequence of small increases in Panama Canal tolls is an indication that the cost difference between going through the Canal and doing the next best thing is often very small.[2]

When asked to evaluate the effects of inflation on the cost of canal operations, Brandes admitted that several toll increases would be necessary over the next twenty-three years just to cover costs. He was hesitant to predict whether such increases would effectively decrease revenue, since the calculations would depend on how fast the cost of canal operations increased and on how well the cost increases matched available alternatives. Brandes did feel that actual or potential revenues would meet the needs of the facility over the next five to ten years, but, beyond that, he could offer the senators "no assurance about the ability of the Canal to maintain itself on a self-supporting basis."[3]

He specifically took issue with the view of "many people in Panama in the Government and other individuals ... that this is going to be a great bonanza to them in terms of revenue. I think they are talking about up to $60 million, something that will increase the Government revenue by 15 to 20 percent. I don't see this myself."[4] While "in the very short run" shippers might have no alternative but to pay whatever the Panamanian authorities demanded, "in the longer run they can make alternative arrangements not to use the Canal. Once they have done so, that Canal traffic is lost for good." Brandes summarized the situation neatly: for Panama, the canal was "a truly vital installation," but for the rest of the world it was "simply a convenience and no more than that."[5]

A newspaper report published thirteen years later confirmed the broad lines of Brandes's analysis. It emphasized that uncertainty about the canal's future, compounded by increased international competition, had produced flat revenue and tonnage figures for the previous several years (1986–1989). During these years the canal commission, still under joint U.S.-Panamanian direction, held toll increases to levels absolutely necessary to maintenance, with revenues roughly equal to expenses. Even so, stemming the loss of traffic to other routes proved impossible. Revenue from canal passage in 1989 was $339 million, roughly the same as three years before. More troubling still was the leveling off of the number of ships passing through the canal, which held steady at 12,000 a year.

Some of the drop-off in the late 1980s could be explained by negative economic trends that could reasonably be expected to reverse themselves: declining U.S. imports of Japanese cars, sluggish grain sales, and slower economic growth in the United States and Japan. But much of the problem was structural: the completion in 1982 of a transisthmian pipeline to handle Alaskan North Slope oil, the development of fittings that permitted the double stacking of containers on railroad freight cars in the United States, and the increasing use of oil supertankers too large to traverse the locks.[6] As table 4–1 illustrates, in more recent years there has been a modest recovery in revenues, but its dimensions are by no means remarkable, particularly taking into account the inflation of the U.S. dollar. Projections for 1997 and 1998 are included.

Unfortunately, revenues alone do not tell the whole story. Though the figures for canal traffic continue to climb, the costs of operation and maintenance and contributions to the capital fund are traversing a far steeper grade. In effect, they threaten to exceed toll revenues altogether. For the fiscal years 1996, 1997, and 1998, the canal commission projects deficits of $2.2 million, $34.5 million, and $69.7 million, respectively. To close the gap, the commission has instituted an 8.2 percent increase in tolls as of January 1, 1997, with another 7.5 percent commencing January 1, 1998—only the seventh such increase since the canal opened in 1914. To improve the profitability of the waterway, the commission decided to include for the first time on-deck container capacity, not merely the size of the carriers, as a basis for

TABLE 4–1
Panama Canal Traffic, 1986–1998

Fiscal Year	Number of Transits	Tolls (millions U.S. $)
1986	13,278	323
1987	13,444	330
1988	13,441	339
1989	13,389	330
1990	13,325	356
1991	14,108	375
1992	14,148	369
1993	13,720	401
1994	14,029	419
1995	15,135	463
1996	13,536	483
1997 (projected)	13,870	487
1998 (projected)	13,900	492

Source: Panama Canal Commission

assessing tolls. This decision led to protests from the Federation of ASEAN Shipowners Associations (FASA) and the Singapore National Shipping Association (SNSA).[7]

Though the commission may have calculated rightly that the current traffic could bear that increase, that may not be true of any or all future increases. At an international conclave of users and potential investors held in Panama City September 7–11, 1997, shippers from around the world warned Panama that excessive tolls hikes would cause them to seek alternative routes. "The canal is not the only way to get to the Far East," declared Gerhard Kurz, president of Mobil Shipping and Transportation and the head of a group that represents most tankers controlled by oil companies. He was joined by Ronald Bergman of the Baltic and International Maritime Council, the largest shipowners association in the world, who insisted that if cargo owners find the canal too expensive, "we will have to start moving their goods by other means.... And there are many ways to ship goods around the world." These warnings were apparently inspired by legislation passed earlier in the year by the Panamanian National Assembly requiring the canal to show a profit once it passed to local control.[8]

That acquisition of the waterway will not in all probability consti-
tute a net gain to the exchequer—notwithstanding legislative fiat—
understandably troubles many Panamanians. A case in point is the
complaint by Fernando Manfredo Jr., first Panamanian canal administrator, that "the non-profit status of the Canal will deprive the country
of potential fiscal revenues on one hand, without providing any additional indirect benefits, such as those enjoyed by the United States on
the other." This amounts to nothing more than arguing that geography
is unfair—that the United States is a big country with far-flung maritime and shipping interests, while Panama is a small country whose
only comparative advantage is its physical location and unique geographical configuration.

Manfredo goes somewhat further, however, in arguing that by
maintaining tolls at the break-even level, Panama would be
"subsidiz[ing] the economy of the United States and other user countries of the Canal without reaping any indirect benefit." To the contrary, he asserts, "the Republic of Panama ... regard[s] the Canal as a
source of revenue."

He also raises a question that, curiously enough, was not satisfac-
torily resolved when the treaties were drafted, namely, whether Panama
even has the right to raise tolls as it sees fit—regardless of the economic consequences. In Manfredo's understanding, the Neutrality Treaty
makes no provision for disagreement over increases, unlike, say, the
rules laid down by the Constantinople Commission, which established
the rules for the Bosphorus Canal, and fails to provide any mechanism
for mediation or arbitration of disputes over rates. "One can only imagine the outcome," Manfredo writes, "should the United States challenge Panama's need to increase tolls for any reason, based either on
legitimacy or appropriateness, of the expenses or the need for capital
program, and so forth." An additional "understanding" introduced in
the Neutrality Treaty by the U.S. Senate allows the United States to
veto toll increases, so that any action taken in this regard by Panama
could be denounced by Washington as a violation of the canal's neutrality. This ability, he writes, forces the Panamanian government to
maintain the canal as a nonprofit enterprise, not only depriving it of
revenues, but making it impossible to find a third party to share in the
management on commercial terms.[9] Actually, Manfredo is only half-
right. While it is true that the United States has run the canal on a
break-even basis as a favor to American shippers and consumers, it is
the hard facts of maritime economics—not political pressures from

Washington—that make it difficult for Panama to increase its revenues from the facility significantly.

Personnel and Maintenance Issues. By the time a Panamanian administrator assumed control of the canal in early 1990, 87 percent of the employees of the company were Panamanian, although they were treated as U.S. civil servants and enjoyed the same benefits. The conditions of their employment had been established in Article 10 of the Carter-Torrijos accords, which prohibited discrimination in hiring on the basis of "nationality, sex or race," and affirmed the right of employees to affiliate with international labor organizations. They were also expected, however, to conform to the minimal performance requirements imposed on government employees in the United States.

Since ratification, the percentage of Panamanians working for the commission has notably increased, from 69.2 percent (1979) to 92 percent (1997). Some 2,000 of the 9,000 employees are expected to retire after 1999. This change may create a vacuum of knowledgeable workers trained to run the facility and force the local authorities to contract out to expatriates.

As an employer, the canal commission has been "an island of meritocracy in a country where nepotism, influence-peddling, and old-boy networks often determine government hiring decisions."[10] One shipping agent put it thus: "Panama has to adapt things to an American system or they have to modify the Panama Canal to fit the Panamanian mode…. The problem is, they do not plug into each other. You've got a Panamanian socket and an American plug."

To resolve this problem, legislation projects replacement of the Panama Canal Commission with a new body, to be known as the Panama Canal Authority (PCA). This agency will consist of a directorate of eleven persons, ten selected by the president of the republic. Nine of the eleven will be subject to confirmation by the Panamanian National Assembly, which will also have the right to nominate a member. Nine of the eleven members will serve fixed terms of nine years, staggered to ensure the board's political independence (Panamanian presidents serve five-year terms and are not eligible for consecutive reelection).[11] The chief operating officer of the PCA, the administrator of the canal, will serve a seven-year term. The PCA will have the right to draw up its own budget, subject to approval or rejection (but not modification) by the National Assembly.[12]

These provisions sound impressive, but many members of the international shipping community remain unconvinced. In Panama, a senior executive of one such concern recently declared, "You have to deal with sudden swings of policy, nepotism, corruption, and laws that look good on paper but are never enforced."[13] His suspicions appear to be amply justified by President Pérez Balladares's decision in late 1997 to pack the canal authority with relatives and political allies: four of the eleven members belong to either his or his wife's family, "including a first cousin, a son-in-law, and the spouses of two other cousins." Other choices include one of the chief fund-raisers of his presidential campaign, "a businessman famous for being embroiled in lawsuits"; two leading members of his Panamanian Revolutionary Party—who held major portfolios in Noriega's puppet governments—and the son of Pérez Balladares's former foreign minister. The designated head of the new authority, Jorge Ritter, minister for canal affairs, has no qualifications as an engineer or a transportation expert. He was the Panamanian ambassador to the United Nations and Colombia during the Noriega period; he is widely alleged to have had links to the Colombian drug cartel. His only claim to the position would seem to be a long-standing personal and political friendship with Pérez Balladares.[14]

The disconnect between the "Panamanian socket" and the "American plug" was obvious as long as ten years ago—even though the canal was still being run by a binational board. Most disquieting of all was the quality of maintenance of those facilities already turned over to the Panamanian government. The most egregious case was that of the Panama railroad, a fifty-mile line that once ferried cargo and passengers across the isthmus and that had been ceded to the Panamanian government immediately after ratification. While the Panamanians did receive this facility in less than mint condition, thanks to a systematic diversion of the funds earmarked for its upkeep as well as the gratuitous expansion of its payrolls, by the mid-1990s the facility was virtually in ruins. It stands as "a cautionary symbol," one journalist reported, "of much that could go wrong for Panama and the United States when the clock strikes midnight at the turn of the century."[15]

Some analysts pointed to the ports of Balboa on the Gulf of Panama and Cristóbal on the Atlantic side as additional reasons for concern. These facilities are among the most valuable industrial resources in the country. Cristóbal handles a large volume of cargo from the duty-free zone established at Colón, while Balboa is a refueling and servicing center for ships using the canal. At least until the ouster of Noriega, Panamanian officials, in the words of the same shipping agent, neglected the ports "completely—with little new equipment, little investment, corruption all over the place. It was disaster. In the last two years [under Noriega] they had a carpetbag approach to everything." The Endara administration was reportedly studying how to rehabilitate the two ports but as of this date had yet to devise a comprehensive plan.[16]

A 1993 newspaper report suggested that even in the canal facility proper there was a marked deterioration in maintenance. The locks, though still managed by the United States, were showing signs of disrepair, causing needless delays in traffic and forcing ships to queue up at canal entrances for periods so long as to cancel out the economic advantage of using the facility. Unidentified "international maritime officials" were quoted as doubting that a country with a population and economy smaller than many American cities could "be expected to run one of the most complex engineering enterprises in the world."

Because they are so specific, some critics should be quoted *in extenso.* One American pilot said, "It is not the same Canal in terms of efficiency and safety that it was when I came here 12 years ago." He complained about growing delays due to malfunctions of the water gates and of the specially designed locomotives ("mules") that pull ships through the locks. He also cited the rotting away of rubber and wooden guards on the sides of the locks, which led to a number of minor accidents, including the denting of ships that cost $50,000 and more to repair.

Adrian Holmes, the operating manager of C. D. Fenton, one of the largest shipping agencies in Panama, put it this way: "Maintenance is a word the Panamanian government has never heard of. The port pilings are deteriorating, causing more ship accidents all the time. The oil pipelines off the docks are leaking. The launches are all in bad repair. The railroad is useless." Holmes remarked that many of his customers, which included Dole, Mobil Oil, and Star Shipping, were contemplating phasing out the use of the canal in favor of a railroad "land bridge" across the continental United States. Another shipping agent was quoted as saying that because efficiency had dropped constantly over the previous ten years, the world shipping community shared the view that "service is deficient."[17]

Although the U.S. representatives on the canal commission tend, perhaps understandably, to be relentlessly upbeat about the quality of canal maintenance, many U.S. officials have proved something less than unequivocal when questioned on the subject by Congress. At a

March 1995 hearing of the House Subcommittee on the Western Hemisphere, Congressman Dan Burton put it to a senior State Department
official that "certainly the change [from U.S. to Panamanian] management cannot result in no difference" at all in the quality of canal maintenance. The response was that "we have a lot of work with the Panamanians to do in the next five years.... But from the standpoint of
operations right now, it is largely in Panamanian hands except for the
top management positions," this last assertion surely beside the point.
Congressman Robert Toricelli cited reports from shippers that there
was a perceptible difference in maintenance and efficiency and asked
the same official directly whether she had "any reason to believe that
this is not the case." The response was that "it is our understanding
that this is not the case." "And the frequency of dredging, the repair of
the locks, the maintenance of the equipment," Congressman Toricelli
pressed, "you consider that it would be equal to the levels of several
years ago?" Again, the answer was somewhat evasive: "Certainly in
recent years, yes."[18]

Presumably, this last remark refers to the businesslike decision of
President Pérez Balladares to earmark for maintenance more than $100
million of the roughly $419 million collected in toll revenues during
1994. Unfortunately, this figure falls far short of what is needed to compensate for neglect during the years of military rule. A U.S. Army Corps
of Engineers report released three years later listed some 830 maintenance tasks that still required immediate attention. Of these, fully 389—
which is to say, 47 percent—had not even been started. They include
such arcane matters as replacing the existing locks machinery, reacti-
vating emergency dams (the upkeep on which has been "abandoned
since 1982"), repairing the concrete around the locks machinery tun-
nel (the work done to date was found "less than desirable"), widening
the Atlantic entrance, and refurbishing the tugboat fleet and the canal
railroad (the "mules"). [19] Although the same report did identify 247
projects already in progress (30 percent) and 194 that had already been
completed (23 percent), President Pérez Balladares chose to interpret
the release of the report on the eve of transfer as a deliberate slap in the
face by the United States. As he put it somewhat petulantly, "The idea,
I guess, would be to hand Panama a canal that would run into problems
shortly afterward." Nonetheless, he subsequently announced a $1 bil-
lion modernization program that encompasses most of the Corps of
Engineers recommendations.[20]

There is no reason to doubt that Panama possesses the engineering or management skills to maintain the canal properly, and what it does not possess, it can easily contract elsewhere. To finance such improvements, however, will require careful stewardship of canal revenues. This, in turn, runs headlong into the country's political culture and its historic patterns of public administration. Traditionally, Panamanians of all classes have regarded government agencies as so much booty to be distributed among followers of the ruling party.[21]

Modernizing Capacity. For some time now, the international shipping community and interested governments have been contemplating ways of modernizing the canal. This prospect was already anticipated in Article 12 of the Carter-Torrijos treaty, which committed the United States not to build an interoceanic route elsewhere in the hemisphere, obliged the United States to study jointly with Panama the possible construction of a sea-level canal on the latter's territory, and granted to the United States the right to add a third lane of locks to the existing canal. This same proviso inspired the United States, Panama, and Japan to establish a Tripartite Commission for Studies on Alternatives to the Panama Canal in 1986. The immediate motivation was the need to resolve the congestion that was causing the facility to lose in excess of $100 million a year (delay imposed on ships waiting to transit the canal was encouraging the use of other routes or modes of transport). But the commission was also concerned that an increasing percentage of the world's fleet consisted of carriers incapable of transiting the existing set of locks. They were likewise impassable for U.S. aircraft carriers.

In July 1992 the commission selected three alternatives for study. One focused on alternative improvements to the existing canal: a highrise lock that would raise Lake Gatún's mean water level to 85–90 feet and a low-rise lock that would maintain the same body of water at 30–55 feet. These modifications could be accomplished relatively quickly. The second was a third set of locks, whose lanes would run adjacent to the existing channels, though wider and deeper. The project would take ten years to complete at a cost of $5.4–8.5 billion, depending on whether one lane or two and whether capable of accommodating vessels of 150 or 250 deadweight tons (DWT). The final alternative was a sea-level canal to be excavated along Panama's Route 10, to run 16 kilometers west of the existing facility and parallel to it. Such an undertaking would take fifteen years to build and cost an estimated $14.2 billion. Both the second and third alternatives presupposed the continuing use of the existing canal, whose utility would be increased by a widening of the Gaillard Cut, the narrow passageway that joins Lake Gatún with the Pacific side (see map).

In its final report released the following year, the commission found that (1) the high-level alternative (HRL), with a single-lane portion in the Gaillard Cut, operating in conjunction with the present canal, and capable of handling 200,000 DWT vessels, would be "marginally feasible"; (2) a one-lane sea-level canal, capable of handling 250,000 DWT vessels, "would not be feasible"; (3) with a widening of the Gaillard Cut, the existing canal could accommodate demand to at least the end of the second decade of the twenty-first century; (4) the high-rise–lock alternative, capable of handling vessels of 150 DWT, would be the "most effective enhancement"; and (5) additional research was needed, "especially in the areas of impacts on the environment and of geomorphological and natural conditions," as well as "a thorough study of a toll structure with a more user-friendly scenario."[22]

Any decision to enhance the existing facility necessarily rests on two considerations. The first is the future political stability of Panama, which would justify the investment of large amounts of money over a relatively long period, with no prospect of recuperation until the improved facility was brought on line. But even given a political universe of perfect tranquility, there is still the tricky calculus of raising enough money through tolls to amortize construction loans without forfeiting significant amounts of traffic in the process. To illustrate the complexity of this point, we have selected the least costly alternative, namely, widening the existing Gaillard Cut.[23] A 1992 report by the Committee on Merchant Marine and Fisheries of the U.S. House of Representatives concentrates on this point.[24] It cites the findings of three different studies. One projected a cost of $400 million (1986 dollars), requiring a tolls surcharge of 10 percent; another anticipated an expenditure of $300 million (1988 dollars), funded by a tolls surcharge of 7 percent; a third did not attempt a cost estimate but predicted an 8.5 percent tolls surcharge. The latter two projections insisted that no construction could begin until the canal authorities were in possession of a two-year funding reserve.

The committee report presented an evaluation of the possibility of starting an eleven-year construction scheme as soon as possible, regardless of long-range traffic projections. In every case, "the costs would be incurred so far in advance," it projected, "that any benefits to Canal users ... clearly reflected negative cost-benefit ratios." This conclusion was particularly troubling because the increasing use of wide-beam vessels that cannot transit the canal will continue to compress its reserve margin. And if the problem of reserve funds is not addressed, "Canal users would be faced after the year 2000 either with the direct impact of a substantial cost to increase capacity on a short-term crash basis, or with the impact of higher CWT and the adverse effect on their shipping schedules."

Regardless of the economic projections, the Panamanian government has decided to go ahead with a widening of the Gaillard Cut. This action would permit the twenty-four-hour passage of the large 100-foot (Panamax) ships, which under present circumstances can negotiate the waterway only during the daylight hours. Increasing demands have moved the termination date—originally scheduled to be completed by 2014—forward to 2005. Fortunately, no advance funding is needed, and the dredging can be done with existing canal resources on a flexible "do as you can" basis. Whether the costs can be recovered through tolls—even with the projected increases—remains an open question, however, as does whether Panama can increase purchases of locomotives and tugboats, as well as improve the locks' hydraulic systems.[25] More ambitious projects await financing, that is, compelling evidence that they can pay for themselves, as well as proof that Panama can insulate the canal facility from political patronage.

Meanwhile, the country is fortunate in at least one sense: it need not fear the construction of alternative routes elsewhere in the isthmus. A combination land-water route through Nicaragua, a conception that predates the canal, has failed to find financing, as has a dry canal through Costa Rica, which contemplated a railroad specially constructed to hold container cargo.[26] In the end, the threat of other, nonisthmian routes can best be kept at bay by a rigorous, businesslike management of the canal facility.

Environmental Issues. At the time of the ratification hearings in 1977–1978, environmental issues received relatively little attention, though they are of crucial relevance to the operation of the canal. As Transportation Secretary Brock Adams explained to the Foreign Relations Committee, without modifications the present canal required 52 million gallons of fresh water to flow out with each transit. "That causes in the present circumstances such a severe water shortage in the dry season," he told the senators, "that they have to often restrict the draft vessels transiting the Canal."

Construction of a third lane of locks would complicate matters further, requiring as much as 100 million gallons per transit. There was simply no way, he avowed, that the Chagrés River Basin could produce so much water. The only alternative—to pump ocean water back into the Central Lake—would seriously compromise the ecosystem by rendering Panama City's fresh water supply brackish. Even discounting the environmental impact, the costs of such a procedure would make it prohibitive; these expenditurers could not be recuperated through increased tolls. A sea-level canal posed even more serious difficulties, the secretary explained, because the tidal flow on the Pacific side is approximately ten feet higher than the Atlantic side and thus expensive barrier dams would have to be built to protect the Central Lake. More to the point, while less fresh water would be required for a sea-level canal, such a facility could not use a gravity flow system.

The senators were somewhat abashed by the information. Given that the existing water supply was not always adequate at certain times of the year and that the number of transits wanting to pass through the canal was bound to increase, "Where," asked Senator Dick Clark, "[will] the fresh water come from?" Secretary Adams turned helplessly to his Assistant Secretary Edward Scott, whose answer is worth recalling in full:

> Let me respond to that, because it is a technical question requiring a technical answer. The canal presently has a water supply improvement program, and it has a lot of dimensions to it. One of the dimensions is that the deeper the cut, the more water you can store in the cut itself. They are looking at seeding clouds and lots of different things, but the point is, those capacity projections were made by a very reliable authority on the canal and are based on all the improvements that are presently being made to the canal to increase water supply. But it nevertheless is true that under present conditions there is a water supply problem.[27]

"Under present conditions there is a water supply problem"—and this was under optimal circumstances, with access to the Lake Gatún watershed closed to squatters by U.S. military personnel. As scientist John Hopkins of the University of California, Santa Barbara, wrote to Senator Claiborne Pell at the time, "Until now the one bright spot in [the Central American] environmental picture has been the Panama Canal Zone." U.S. regulations "have prohibited settling and forest cutting in much of the area so that a lot of relatively undisturbed forest remains…. The pressure on this land will be immense and immediate once it is handed over to the Republic of Panama." Hopkins was particularly concerned about plans to designate the Pipeline Road area as a park, as well as to incorporate the Madden Forest Preserve into the Panamanian park system.

> If the Pipeline Road preserve is not actually set up with effective protection before the land is handed over [he wrote], on ratification of the treaty it will be too late. A road is already there and the common experience in Central America is road equals settlers and food gatherers equals total destruction of the forest in a very short space of time. Reliance on this proposal for protection of the area would be, at best, a very risky step.[28]

These concerns have proved remarkably prophetic. Panama's needs for water have increased exponentially since 1978. The Gatún and Alahuela reservoirs provide the 52 million tons required daily for ships to transit the canal, but they must also provision Panama City and Colón, where more than half the country's population resides. Of the two, Alahuela is the greatest importance, since it provides 2.8 billion gallons of water a day. Slightly more than half—58 percent—is released through sluices to the sea, enabling thirty-two ships to transit the canal. Some 33 percent is diverted to hydroelectric facilities, 4 percent lost in preventing release, and 6 percent is consumed as drinking water. Unfortunately, these amounts fall short of Panama's future needs. By the year 2000, almost 4 billion gallons a day must be extracted.

There is little likelihood of this target being met because the entire ecosystem of the Chagrés River Basin has been steadily deteriorating. The most serious problem is deforestation. Whereas in 1952 some 85 percent of the area was covered by forests, by 1983 the figure had fallen to 30 percent (by some estimates, to 20 percent). While there are no accurate figures for the rate of deforestation, various extrapolations suggest that the basin may be virtually denuded by the twenty-second century. Deforestation has a negative impact on rainfall and, even more important, fosters erosion and the buildup of sediment in the lakes, which create problems for navigation. Frequent dredging is expensive and introduces delays that detract from the canal's competitiveness with other forms of transoceanic shipment.

During the years following the ratification of the treaties, successive Panamanian governments found it increasingly difficult to prevent massive peasant migration into areas formerly protected by the Canal Zone authorities. Although the Carter-Torrijos treaties specifically enjoined the Panamanian government to ensure that sufficient water was available to operate the canal, no administration has been willing (or able) to apply a consistent policy of environmental enforcement. The result has been an explosion of slash-and-burn agriculture—the only kind squatters can readily practice without access to credit and advanced technology—followed by the conversion of many forested areas into grazing areas for cattle. By one estimate as recently as 1993, this was the fate of some *90 percent* of all deforested land in the area. Though the worst alternative from an environmental point of view, it has received decided support from the Panamanian government, since it provides a ready supply of meat for Panama's urban population.

The invasion of squatters onto land formerly held in trust for the environment has not resolved the problems of Panama's landless peasantry, since over time slash-and-burn techniques have rendered much of it unusable for anything but grazing, the province of wealthy ranchers. Having destroyed their own source of subsistence, peasants now have no choice but to migrate to Panama's overcrowded urban areas. Meanwhile, the mining of primary materials for construction and industrialization has led to the increasing contamination of the water supply for Panama City and Colón, as has a promiscuous approach to the construction of roads, particularly "summer shortcuts," a major factor in land erosion and the silting up of water courses.

In retrospect, it seems remarkable that so little attention was paid to these problems when the treaties were drafted, and even more inexplicable that the Panamanian government so readily entered into obligations that it was wholly unprepared to meet. One Panamanian student of the subject argues that it is time to revise the treaties, at least to the extent of requiring the canal commission to make some sort of contribution to maintenance of the ecosystem. As things stand now, not a single cent of the roughly $400 million–$500 million transit fees collected by the canal is allocated to protecting the basin; for their part, urban consumers in Panama City and Colón pay only a small charge to cover the cost of making the water potable. He suggests imposing a toll surcharge of three cents per ton (which would produce about $9 million revenue per year) to meet the challenge, and raising utility charges for city dwellers.

Presumably, a surcharge this modest would not compromise the canal's capacity to compete with other routes. But whether Panamanians themselves are ready to face increased water charges is less clear. Quite apart from the serious hardship that higher rates would impose on lower-income families, there is no widespread understanding of the problem. Panama's environmental organizations are small and poorly funded, and they lack political influence.[29] At the time of the treaties, Panama did not have a comprehensive system of environmental law—and does not still. Those laws on the books are not enforced, and generally Panamanians do not grasp the logic of environmental concerns. As the same Panamanian environmentalist put it, "Regardless of their class or level of education, Panamanians consider their natural resources to be inexhaustible."[30]

At the level of Panama's leadership, discourse on this subject has not been particularly illuminating. At the international congress to discuss the future of the canal (September 7–11, 1997), Minister Ritter was pointedly asked about the supply of fresh water for the facility. His response covered every aspect of the subject except the one most relevant to the question. He pointed with pride to the creation of an "interinstitutional mechanism between government agencies [which] forces the nongovernmental organizations and civilian associations to partake of our efforts to protect the water basin." From there, he jumped to saying that "the Canal has never shut down due to a water shortage"—true enough but beside the point. Ritter went on: "The water basin ... exceeds what any of us imagine.... it occupies an area equivalent to 50 percent of the provinces of Panama.... 320,000 hectares of water basin that all Panamanians and government and nongovernmental agencies alike must commit to protecting." If Ritter's response is at all symptomatic of the current state of attention to environmental issues, canal users—and, indeed, responsible Panamanians—have reason to be seriously concerned.[31]

Meanwhile, Panamanian politicians and environmental groups are demanding that the United States clean up 11,000 acres formerly used for weapons testing and practice. Such a project would cost hundreds of millions of dollars. The United States regards this request as unreasonable and unrealistic. Quite apart from the fact that the Carter-Torrijos treaties do not mandate such action (Article 6, section 2 of the canal treaty is remarkably vague, merely calling for joint consultation "to mitigate the adverse environmental impacts that might result from their respective actions pursuant to this Treaty"), what the Panamanians are insisting on would be technologically impractical and work at cross-purposes with other, more pressing environmental agendas. "Technology today makes it impractical to clean out these areas one hundred percent," Colonel David Hunt, director of the U.S. Army's Center of Treaty Implementation, explained. "We will do sweeps and try to remove as much as we can, but we can't tear down every tree in the jungle." To get rid of all the old ordinance, he added, "you'd destroy the watershed."[32]

Defense of the Canal

The Strategic Context. For many years, the Panama Canal amounted to something of a totem in U.S. strategic thinking, inasmuch as it automatically elevated disturbances anywhere in the region to the status of potentially serious threats. Any untoward event in any of the circum-Caribbean, including Cuba, could be interpreted—rightly or wrongly—as threatening in some way to the security of the waterway. Much rhetoric of American policy was extravagant in this regard, particularly during and after World War II. In fact, the canal has been remarkably free of serious threats throughout its history; it has been closed only a single day since its opening in 1914—by U.S. authorities following the American invasion of 1989.

That much said, one can hardly regard a broader concern for canal security as a frivolous matter. U.S. control of one of the world's two most important interoceanic waterways allowed it to project considerable power and influence in the international security arena and guaranteed "efficient use of logistic facilities and training centers on all three coasts of the United States." This position also allowed the United States to maintain a one-and-a-half rather than two-ocean navy, "directly or indirectly saving [the U.S. taxpayer] billions of dollars."[33] The canal remains one of the world's crucial "choke-points" for oceanborne traffic, controlling a significant portion of international commerce.

From 1903 through the end of World War II, the operative considerations of U.S. strategy in Panama were assured access to the canal and denial of the same to real or potential enemies. This situation called for the construction of traditional military fortifications and of land, sea, and air bases. During the cold war, U.S. objectives were enlarged to include the somewhat more elusive task of containing communism,[34] though the physical protection of the canal facility remained a priority of the highest order. It remains so even today.

For many years, U.S. forces stationed in Panama and the Panamanian Defense Forces (FDP) equitably shared defense responsibilities. The Americans provided industrial-type plant protection for the canal and adjoining facilities and also trained its own countersabotage and counterreaction forces, while the FDP operated within the territory of the republic—concentrating on crowd control, counterinsurgency, and, in recent years, frontier security (that is, monitoring the country's northern border to prevent illegal immigration from poorer Central American countries, particularly El Salvador and Nicaragua).

As noted in chapter 2, the ratification hearings of 1977–1978 devoted an extraordinary amount of time to exploring what provisions the treaties made for the defense of the canal. Since the end of the cold war, however, there has been some controversy over whether these concerns are not outdated. Colonel Max Manwaring put it this way: "The logic of the dialogue regarding the strategic value of the Panama Canal is simple: no threat, no strategic value. Even if there were a threat, however, there is no defense. *Ergo*, the Canal has no strategic value." [35] One might just as easily suggest that the willingness of the United States to surrender the facility in 1978 in and of itself heavily discounts the strategic value of the facility. If the canal were really all that important, would Washington have been so obliging in giving it up in the first place? [36]

Whether the Carter administration's willingness to subscribe to the canal treaties was a well-considered adjustment to declining geopolitical threats or rather—as its critics often claimed—a tragic strategic miscalculation, in retrospect it is difficult to see how anyone could have believed that a Panamanian force could defend the canal in the event—likely or not—of a serious military challenge. [37] Some Panamanian officials have not found this particularly troubling. "I do not see any threat to the canal," Administrator Fernando Manfredo told the press shortly after assuming his position in 1990, "because nobody would stand to gain by destroying it." No army, he added, no matter how large, could effectively counter a determined terrorist threat anyway. [38] For his part, President Endara's Foreign Minister Julio Linares has stated that "defense ... must be based on neutrality," not military force. [39] Attempts to "militarize" the canal would serve no strategic purpose but, even worse, would introduce the germs of a new dictatorship. [40] Panama's National Police could "protect" the canal, declared Vice-President Ricardo Arias Calderón, but to "defend" it clearly exceeds the country's capacity; the United States, he reminded his compatriots, spent $750 million a year doing that very thing, which exceeded income from the facility by $250 million—clearly not a feasible project.[41]

The Panamanian public seems to share these views, though probably more because of unpleasant memories of the Noriega regime than any considered evaluation of the country's strategic needs or its financial capacity. Polls consistently show no nostalgia for the revival of the Panamanian army in any form and are of a piece with the consistent desire to see U.S. military personnel remain in the country after the year 2000.[42] Indeed, so strong are these feelings that President Ernesto Pérez Balladares has resisted pressures from within his Democratic Revolutionary Party to reconstitute a Panamanian army, notwithstanding the fact that one of its constituencies is made up of cashiered officers of the former FDP.

The result is an anomaly. As canal treaties negotiator and former minister of justice Juan Materno Vásquez has put it, regardless of what the documents themselves may say, without an army Panama cannot share the defense of the canal with the United States. It must rely on American forces to "protect the domestic order" in Panama itself. "The country which declares [itself] permanently neutral and assumes its defense with U.S. cooperation," he warns, "in effect withdraws from that pact, leaving the remaining members of the international community, who have signed the pact together with the U.S., with the exclusive responsibility of defending the Canal."[43] Thus far, this has been the case.

Changing Threats. But against what or whom is the canal to be defended? This question is particularly pregnant in light of the disappearance of the Soviet Union and the hobbling of Fidel Castro's capacity for trouble making in the region. The answer would seem to be the criminal elements within Panama allied to the Colombian drug cartels. This, at any rate, is the scenario worked out by a high-level study group at the U.S. Department of Defense, released to the press in February 1992. Charged with defining seven hypothetical situations that required strategic planning, the group imagined a situation in which right-wing elements of the former national police in alliance with "former drug-dealing [FDP] leaders who have connections to narcoterrorist elements of the Revolutionary Armed Forces of Colombia" threaten to close down the Panama Canal unless the local government hands over power there.[44]

While the scenario may be a bit far-fetched, it reflects the emergence of a cluster of new security issues—drugs, international crime, terrorism, and money laundering—that, while in and of themselves not necessarily threatening to the canal, are not particularly reassuring, either. The issues are not all that new. Even during the Torrijos era there were persistent rumors of links between Panamanian government officials and the international criminal underworld, rumors that drew sustenance from the country's transformation in the 1970s into a major center of offshore banking. Accusations became more pointed during the reign of Noriega and, in part, led to (or, at least, were used to justify) the invasion of 1989.

The installation of the Endara government by U.S. forces did not significantly improve the situation. As a result, in 1994 the White House found it necessary to sidestep certification of Panama altogether.[45] Senator John Kerry, who then chaired the narcotics subcommittee of the Senate Foreign Relations Committee, returned from a visit in frank despair. "We replaced a system of organized crime under Noriega," he declared, "with a system of disorganized crime under the current government." And he went on to say:

> Panama is again moving huge quantities of cocaine through the Colón Free Zone to the United States. Its judicial system is frustrating swift prosecution of traffickers; and its financial and banking system are an open invitation for criminals to launder money.[46]

In this connection Panama's close geographical proximity to Colombia is particularly troubling. The province of Darien, which borders on the northernmost tip of Colombia's Choco Province, is a wild, sparsely populated area, home to clandestine labs and airfields. From here Colombia's troubles—drug trafficking, terrorism, and counterterrorism—easily spill into Panama itself. A case in point is Puerto Abadía, a town of 700 souls. Though formally on the Panamanian side, it is populated by people of Colombian origin and patrolled by twenty-five Panamanian police officers. According to President Endara's Attorney-General Rogelio Cruz, since at least 1988 Colombian drug traffickers have been smuggling their product—as well as millions of dollars in cash—through Puerto Abadía for transshipment through Panama or laundering through Panamanian banks. Some sense of the magnitude of the problem is afforded by the figures he gave; $1 million was transferred to Panama during the last three days of August 1991 alone.[47]

Clashes between Colombian paramilitary groups and rebels on

Panamanian soil are taking place with increasing frequency, with the local authorities powerless to do anything about it. Indeed, by the summer of 1997 the situation had become so serious that Panamanian authorities were granting permission for Colombian Army troops to camp in Darien Province and conduct operations against rebels who had taken refuge there.[48] While Government and Justice Minister Raúl Montenegro repeatedly insisted that "nothing has happened on the border with Colombia," in the same breath he announced a new $12 million security program for Darien under the control of the National Police. A sweep of the area (rather euphemistically titled Operation Peace and Security) was intended to neutralize Colombian guerrilla and paramilitary groups. Montenegro also announced that a study was underway to improve landing strips, helicopter landing sites, and communications for Darien Province—none of which sounded as if the area was merely a placid provincial backwater.[49]

National Police Director José Luís Sosa offered a far more frank assessment, telling the press the following day that crime is "practically uncontrollable in the Darien area" and that Operation Peace and Security could be extended indefinitely if the situation warranted it.[50] A few days later, while still denying that the situation was serious, Montenegro allowed as how police reinforcements would remain in Darien as long as the circumstances required. For his part, *La Prensa* publisher Roberto Eisenmann, Jr., raised the more troubling question: if Colombia, with a well-trained army of 140,000 men, could not secure that country's borders, what hope was there for Panama, whose constitution forbade its remilitarization and whose policemen had enough trouble fulfilling their humdrum duties in downtown Panama City?[51]

The growth of international crime in Panama—whether inspired by drug trafficking or something else—is troubling from the point of view of both the country's general political stability and future investor confidence. It also shades imperceptibly into the gray areas of political terrorism, although only one such incident has been reported. This involved the 1994 explosion in midair of a commuter plane outside Colón, an incident in which twenty-one people, several of them American citizens, were killed. At first, U.S. and Panamanian police authorities were unsure whether the plane was destroyed by technical deficiencies or sabotage, but an offshoot of the Hizballah terrorist group in the Middle East soon issued a statement linking the event to the recent bombing of the Jewish Center in Buenos Aires. As one U.S. official remarked, this was "well before aviation experts had determined that the plane had, in fact, been bombed."[52]

U.S. defense planners are mainly concerned with the safety of the canal rather than random acts of criminality in Panama, however ideologically inspired. Insofar as terrorist attacks are concerned, all sorts of eventualities are imaginable, though—given the end of the cold war—not all are probable. Those in the United States who favor some sort of residual American military presence in Panama are sometimes inclined to brandish what can only be described as worst-case scenarios. In the congressional hearings cited above, Congressman Burton mentioned the possibility that "if the Gatún Dam was blown for some reason, it would depress the water levels in that lake, and make it virtually impossible to transit the canal ... with very little difficulty, some charges of dynamite or plastic explosives could render it impassable."[53]

To this, General Frederick C. Smith, principal deputy assistant secretary of defense for international security affairs, responded that "in terms of threat assessment, it is a low chance." When pressed as to whether the canal could be "defended ... from external threats externally," he answered in the affirmative: "We do have other naval assets available [in the region] that could defend against that type of threat." One of his uniformed colleagues intervened to say that the residual U.S. military presence in Panama "does not necessarily do anything but deter some sort of internal threat. Even with all the policemen in New York, they were still able to bomb the Trade Center. But there is a certain amount of deterrence that you get from our presence there on the ground."

These remarks led Congressman Toricelli onto a more interesting tack, namely, that while "you cannot guard against a terrorist activity," there are other invisible but more tangible benefits to the U.S. presence. "Staying with the comparison of the World Trade Center," he continued, "the terrorist also knows you commit the act, but you are also not going to get away [with it] because those forces are there to apprehend. That must be part of a deterrent operation." He then asked whether it would be correct "to say that the net result of American withdrawal of forces, if it were to become complete ... without that deterrence effect there, w[ould] be less security against terrorist activities." The officer replied, "Yes, sir, I agree that you lose the deterrent effect."[54]

The Public Force. To replace both the declining American military presence and the old Panama Defense Force, officials of both countries have set about creating something more nearly resembling the Costa

Rican model of a national police. This body, known as the Public Force (PF), consists of three elements: the National Police (the largest component), the National Air Service (replacing the old Panamanian Air Force), and the National Maritime Service (superseding the old Panamanian Navy). The commander in chief of the Public Force is the president of the republic, rather than a serving officer, although on a day-to-day basis these commands are under the authority of the Ministry of Government and Justice. The Judicial Technical Police (PTJ), responsible for criminal investigations, has, since 1992, been subordinated to the office of the attorney general. The fate of the old FDP was sealed in October 1994, when the Legislative Assembly approved an amendment to the Constitution banning the creation of a conventional military force.

From the beginning, the United States has supported the Public Force with significant amounts of training and equipment, primarily from the Justice Department's International Criminal Investigations Training and Assistance Program. This support included the expenditure (as of 1994) of $30 million to train and equip Panamanian troops for canal protection, a force of some 700 people. The United States has also undertaken to prepare specialized units (SWAT teams, hostage rescue teams, etc.) to deal with the problem of urban terrorism.[55] At the same time, security spending by Panama itself has risen to rather considerable levels. As of 1994, some $500 million had been expended in this area, a whopping 36 percent of the government's budget. On an average annual basis, this was slightly more than the amounts expended by the military government, which was in the habit of disbursing about $105 million a year in its final days. Such outlays have made possible the creation of a National Police force of 12,500 people. Even so, these people were reportedly capable of providing coverage for only 55 percent of the areas requiring police protection.[56]

Quite apart from sheer numbers, there is some question as to whether the Public Force can meet Panama's immediate security needs. Since 1990, there has been a proliferation of private security companies to provide protection for industrial plants, businesses, even residential neighborhoods. Nonetheless, in the years since Noriega's fall, there has been a quantum leap in the number of bank robberies and other crimes, such as to throw "business and private sectors in our nation in a state of alarm." Part of the problem is one of leadership—during the first two years, the PF had six different directors; part is a lack of equipment and weapons, as well as poor salaries and fringe benefits, which have encouraged corruption and laggard performance on the job.[57]

A long and traumatic experience with the military has led to widespread public suspicion of all security agencies. One poll—admittedly not recent—may exaggerate these fears, since it was taken shortly after an abortive coup attempt against the Endara administration by Colonel Eduardo Herrera Hassan, a former FDP officer, in December 1990. (The affair was suppressed by U.S. troops at the request of the Panamanian government.) Nonetheless, at that stage, 70 percent of those surveyed did not trust the National Police, with 76 percent registering no confidence whatever in the Judicial Technical Police. Slightly more than 54 percent thought that the new body was actually the FDP "in civilian disguise," while only 32 percent thought otherwise. Only 49 percent thought that the government had full control over its security forces.[58] Presumably these gloomy perceptions have lifted in subsequent years, at least to the extent that the Pérez Balladares administration has gone a long way toward assuring Panamanians that the PF does not represent, in embryo, a new version of the hated National Guard. Whether the apparent disappearance of a praetorian threat to civilian rule has been matched by increased police efficiency is quite another matter. Even if it has, a force designed to cover the urban areas where most Panamanians live cannot be expected to assume new and more ambitious tasks on the country's southern frontier. This is one of the many issues that has encouraged some Panamanians and Americans to contemplate revision of the Carter-Torrijos treaties, a point to which we now turn.

5

★

The Revisionist Temptation

F or many decades, Panama has been one of the major venues of
U.S. military and naval presence overseas, home to ten major
and more than two dozen minor defense installations. These include Albrook Air Station, Fort Amador, Fort Clayton, Fort Davis, Fort
Espinar, Howard Air Force Base, Fort Kobbe, Quarry Heights, and
Rodman Naval Station. Panama has long been the headquarters of the
U.S. Southern Command (SouthCom), whose responsibilities now include the entire Western Hemisphere south of Mexico, and of the School
of the Americas, a training facility for officers from Latin American
countries run by the U.S. Army. Fort Sherman houses a jungle warfare
training school, and Galeta Island off the Atlantic side of the canal
serves as a major naval intelligence facility.

The Carter-Torrijos treaties clearly and unambiguously establish
that after the year 2000 no U.S. troops or military installations will
exist anywhere in the Republic of Panama. As a result, since 1979
some twenty bases large and small have been closed, and their properties surrendered to the local authorities. In addition, the U.S. Army has
moved the School of the Americas to Fort Benning, Georgia, and has
begun relocating the SouthCom headquarters to Miami. As of mid-1997,
among the major facilities only Galeta Island, Fort Clayton, Quarry
Heights, Howard and Rodman Naval Bases, Fort Sherman, and Fort
Kobbe remained under U.S. authority.[1] From a high of 12,000 troops in
pretreaty days, roughly 4,500 troops are now stationed there, though

the number will probably be smaller by the time these words reach print because, in many cases, Washington has been moving ahead of schedule to fulfill its treaty commitments.

The expeditious dismantling of these installations underscores in the most persuasive possible fashion the apparently firm decision of both governments to abide by Carter-Torrijos regarding the closing of U.S. bases. Certainly, no American administration has chosen to suggest otherwise publicly, and, until recently, every Panamanian government since 1977, whether military or civilian, has rejected—sometimes vociferously—the idea of a residual U.S. military presence anywhere in the national territory.

But these are not the only relevant facts. Over the years, it has become increasingly difficult to ignore a rising background clamor in both countries calling for a new arrangement that would allow some American troops to remain. Moreover, nothing in Carter-Torrijos specifically forbids a new treaty that would address this issue; an additional protocol to the original documents signed by both presidents actually contemplates the possibility. This understanding, reached at ratification, is the entering wedge for revision.[2]

Forces and Motives of U.S. Revisionism

In the United States, the revisionist forces are small in number but strategically well placed. They include members of Congress who opposed Carter-Torrijos in the first place, such as Senator Jesse Helms, chairman of the Committee on Foreign Relations, as well as House conservatives close to the military establishment, most notably Congressmen Philip Crane, Gerald Solomon, and James Sensenbrenner. As early as 1979, a sense of the Congress resolution called on the U.S. government to enter into negotiations with a view to maintaining a residual military presence in Panama. Since the end of Panama's military regime in 1989–1990, members of both houses of Congress have repeatedly put the subject on the legislative agenda. In 1991, for example, the Senate urged the president to negotiate a base rights agreement in its versions of H.R. 2508, as well as in the foreign aid and defense authorization bills for the 1992 and 1993 fiscal years. Since 1995, four specific resolutions in the same sense have been introduced and referred to the Committee on International Relations or the Committee on National Security.[3]

A commitment to a residual U.S. military presence in Panama is likewise shared by one of the oldest and most influential nongovernmental organizations in the United States, the Atlantic Council. The report of its blue-ribbon commission, made public in July 1996, called for the two governments to "reach a new agreement for U.S. access to [military and naval] facilities in Panama after 1999." Such an instrument "could provide important benefits to both countries, strengthen bilateral trust and friendship and set the stage for a lasting cooperative relationship into the 21st century." To this end, the U.S. Congress was urged to be prepared to increase additional funding of about $200 million a year, as well as increase the contemplated ceiling in armed forces personnel.[4]

The commission, jointly chaired by General Andrew Goodpaster (U.S. Army, retired) and Panamanian businessman J. J. Vallarino, included distinguished figures from both countries. The Americans who signed on to the report included David C. Acheson, president of the council; former congressman Michael Barnes; former U.S. ambassadors to Panama Dean Hinton, Ambler Moss, and Robert M. Sayre; former army secretaries Stephen Ailes and Stanley Resor; and former Pennsylvania governor Raymond Shafer. Only two of forty-nine American members of the commission dissented from its findings, one from a conservative, the other from a liberal, perspective: Everett Ellis Briggs, former ambassador to Panama, and Peter Hakim, president of the Inter-American Dialogue. To the extent that a fairly arcane foreign policy issue can have an establishment position, revision of Carter-Torrijos has moved beyond the populist-conservative ideological chapel to a kind of mainstream respectability.

Over the past two decades, the Defense Department has gone out of its way to insist that it wholeheartedly embraces Carter-Torrijos and that there is no difference of opinion between itself and the Department of State on a residual presence in Panama. Emblematic of its public position is the statement of General Barry McCaffrey, commander in chief of the U.S. Southern Command (1994–1996), to the effect that while the U.S. presence there "does serve a number of purposes which are enormously beneficial to the region," "there are no vital U.S. national security interests at stake in Panama. We do not have to be here to carry out our responsibilities under the treaty, or to remain engaged in the region." [5]

Nonetheless, it is no secret that some U.S. military agendas would be best served by a residual presence in Panama. These reappear in staff studies, academic theses, and congressional testimony by retired officers. What follows is a catalogue of arguments culled from a representative sample of such documents.[6]

Broad Strategic Views. Those favoring retention of a site that has served a multitude of legitimate military and naval purposes for more than eight decades will not have to look hard to find strategic rationales to justify their position. Some arguments, however, rather transparently mask a strong military-bureaucratic bias to hold onto a desirable duty assignment by deploying vague, sometimes grandiose concepts. "Retentions of an advance base in Panama," one source held, "would strengthen U.S. capability for timely projection of military power throughout the region."[7] "Even a small forward-stationed force can offer a range of benefits," Col. John A. Cope, U.S. Army, retired, claimed. He continued:

> It underwrites regional and Panamanian stability—our first concern—in a very unique and personal way; signals U.S. commitment to cooperative security among hemispheric friends, particularly in the Caribbean basin; provides a visible reminder to those who would threaten our interests; plays an active role in peacetime policy support; and provides timely initial response capabilities in the event of a natural disaster or the need to support diplomacy....
>
> A small U.S. presence remaining in Panama sends a symbolic message to a range of different audiences. As U.S. forces in Europe continue to demonstrate a strong psychological as well as physical commitment to that area of significant national interest, a comparable stationing of forces in Panama makes a similar low-key statement to the inter-American community of nations, particularly those beyond the Caribbean Basin that are so hard to see from the United States.

The retired officer concluded, "It is important that [the Defense Department] be seen as wanting to remain effective in its regional activities and seeking to better understand the region, its culture and language."[8]

For others, the U.S. presence in Panama affords strategic advantages of a more concrete nature. These include reduced flying time for SouthCom officials who visit other Latin American countries or bring officers from those same countries to the headquarters in Panama City; the existence of a complex of commissaries, hospitals, communications, and logistical facilities built up over decades; and, perhaps most important of all, a secure airport. "Sensitive aircraft such as the Aerial Warning and Control System (AWACS)," one officer told an American scholar, "have to land at secure airfields, not international airports. Howard Air Force Base is cheap, convenient, and cost effective," since the U.S. military does not have to pay landing fees there.[9]

Drugs. Another line of argument emphasizes Panama's central location. It is a natural base from which to fight both drug production and trafficking in Northern South America and the circum-Caribbean. Underpinning this approach is the conviction that drugs pose too large a problem to be left to local police forces, since they lack the appropriate weaponry or adequate geographical reach, and that the most effective form of drug enforcement requires joint service exercises, presumably in, or coordinated from, Panama itself. This view also assumes that a lack of vigorous U.S. military involvement in the problem from within the area itself will cause Latin counterparts to lose interest in the problem, in turn threatening stable democracies and emerging market economies throughout the region.

In all of this Panama "cannot be replaced," according to one military intellectual, who explained to a congressional committee that

> If you had to move the aircraft from Howard [Air Force Base] to the United States, we are talking about an additional probably 8 hours, 2,000 miles distance. There is a real increase in sortie rate to maintain surveillance over the region that we have today, and a major cost increase. There would be a great deal of congressional encouragement to decrease the cost increase, I am sure, because it would be extremely expensive to do what we are doing now from Panama.
>
> If you decrease costs by cutting back your flights from the United States, in addition to no presence in Panama, the signal that we send to countries in the region, and to adversaries in the narcotics business, is rather significant. The United States has taken a step backwards. We are not really serious about what we are doing to counter the flow of illegal drugs.
>
> By taking the [Southern] command out of Panama, you lose a driving force in regional coordination to energize efforts to move after the drug lords. If the Command leaves Panama, you would have a deflation in our implementation

of the counternarcotics strategy that would be very difficult to replace.[10]

Of particular importance in the fight against drugs is Howard Air Force Base, the most important U.S. facility in Panama because it has a secure runway, essential for surveillance purposes. Without Howard, the cost of deploying AWACS on counternarcotics missions would increase dramatically and would pose new logistical problems. If the mission had to leave from the continental United States, it would expend considerably more fuel and would be forced to pay landing fees. Further, many Latin American governments might find it politically inexpedient to permit their territories to be used for such missions, at least on a continuous basis. Finally, even if these two problems were overcome and ready access gained at airports throughout the region, satisfying local political requirements might require relying on inferior tower facilities and fuels of a lower grade than needed.[11]

A 1997 Senate staff report also singled out Rodman Naval Station as particularly useful in the war against drugs, since it is home to the U.S. Navy's Small Craft Instruction and Technical Training School, which offers courses on all aspects of maintenance for boats used in "brown water" (island and riverine) operations, precisely the kinds of activities currently employed in many Latin American countries to combat narcotics trafficking.[12]

Communications. The same report cited Galeta Island as a vital communications facility "important principally for search and rescue operations," along with Corozal on the Pacific side of the Panama Canal. The latter houses "the main communication hub for collection and distribution of information to all US forces, not just in Panama, but in the entire region," operated on a round-the-clock basis. Theoretically, the report conceded, routing this traffic might be accomplished through the facilities of the Panamanian national telephone company (National Institute of Telecommunications—INTEL). INTEL, however, "is not comparable to US standards ... cannot acquire the equipment, materials, and resources needed to provide adequate and timely maintenance operation," and its routing and rerouting capabilities for existing traffic within its network are saturated. "More important," it concluded, "INTEL cannot provide secured/classified communication services for the US military in Panama nor can it provide satellite communication ... for US military throughout the entire hemisphere."[13]

Increased Costs and Logistics of Humanitarian and Civic Action Programs. Panama is the center of operations originating at Fort Kobbe, home to the Theater Equipment and Maintenance Site (TEAMS). TEAMS consists of prepositioned military equipment and supplies used for disaster relief and humanitarian and civic action programs. Such supplies would have to be relocated to the United States, thus increasing the costs of transport, or to other Latin American countries, where the United States would have to pay for landing facilities and temporary storage facilities, "including perishable items which require refrigeration facilities."

For many years, the U.S. military has been conducting humanitarian and civic action programs in a wide variety of Latin American countries. Without the TEAMS facility at Kobbe, it could still do so in Central America but probably not in South America. From U.S. bases, moving a mission and its supplies to parts of Central America takes approximately three–four days, but five–six to reach areas in South America. Particularly without Howard AFB, with its sophisticated landing facilities, the total transit costs would likely increase, effectively bringing an end to many, if not most, of these missions.

A decrease in humanitarian missions would have three deleterious results. First, U.S. troops, particularly units of the Army Reserve and National Guard, would have fewer occasions for vital training exercises. Second, the United States would lose the opportunity to demonstrate to Latin Americans the wholesome role that the citizen-soldier can play in society and to hold up for emulation the U.S. model of civil-military relations. Third, U.S. military influence would diminish increasingly in a southern direction, since cost factors would effectively eliminate venues such as Paraguay, Uruguay, and even Bolivia.[14]

Difficulties of Replicating Panamanian Facilities. Fort Sherman provides excellent opportunities for jungle training that probably could not be found elsewhere, particularly since the closing of U.S. bases in the Philippines. Additionally, Sherman affords a unique possibility of year-round training in road building for U.S. engineer battalions. This situation benefits not only the units but the fortunate Panamanians who live in areas where their government has not seen fit to engage in public works. The operations also act as a training theater for medical service battalions of both U.S. active and reserve units.

As a result, Panama is the largest recipient of U.S. humanitarian and civic action projects in Latin America. According to one U.S. government source, between 1992 and 1995 alone, the U.S. military on assignment there built 301 schools and ninety-two health clinics, improved 400 roads, and built sixty-two bridges. In the same period, it provided medical treatment free of charge to 93,600 patients, dental treatment to 23,031, and periodic medical evacuation assistance (nine in 1995 alone). Such activities endear the United States to the Panamanian public, particularly those living in remote rural areas.[15]

Finally, until quite recently a favorite argument for remaining in Panama was the inadequacy of alternative facilities at Soto Cano, Honduras. Originally established as a forward base in the Nicaraguan civil war, Soto Cano is home to 1,100 U.S. Army and Air Force personnel assigned to counternarcotics activity throughout Central America. It is also used for periodic exercises by visiting U.S. reserve units. Despite the U.S. presence there since 1983, however, there is no formal basing agreement with the local government, and the installation itself bears all the marks of its provisional nature.

The prospect of having to withdraw from Panama, however, has led to a rapid upgrading of what was originally a minor facility. Expansion of the runway now makes is possible to land the C-5, our largest plane, and talks are underway with the Honduran government concerning an increased presence, including a status of forces agreement. It is still true, however, that Honduras, the poorest country in Central America, offers few diversions and amenities, certainly nothing comparable to what is available in Panama itself. Understandably, even U.S. reservists are not enthusiastic about spending their two weeks of summer training there.

Asymmetries and Paradoxes of Panamanian Revisionism

Whereas in the United States the subject of a residual military presence in Panama is of interest only to defense specialists, policy analysts, and some members of Congress, in Panama itself the issue lies at the heart of the country's continuing debate over its national identity. Given the nature of Panama's political culture, the discussion itself has been rather unsatisfying and somewhat inconclusive. Without the benefit of the polls cited in chapter 3, one would never know from reading the media, for example, the degree to which the Panamanian public has been open to the idea of a new treaty allowing at least some American troops to remain in the country after the year 2000.

This apparent paradox invites further discussion. Nationalism in

Panama operates in a dialectical fashion. It can appear to be a volatile element that, apparently spontaneously, bubbles up from the urban mob and forces politicians to respect its emotive force. At other times, the concept is merely the most lethal tool at the disposal of the political class when attempting to score points against one another in the game of "more Panamanian than thou." The issue of American bases is the point at which both these aspects intersect. It also touches deeply the Panamanian collective psyche on two crucial counts. One, an American military presence assures the country's permanent claims to the attention of the world's only superpower and thus raises its regional and international status. Second, to invite the Americans unambiguously to remain (through a national plebiscite, no less) all but invalidates the country's claims to independence and therefore—in symbolic terms—lowers its regional and international status. Because the politicians understand this better than the general public, few of them— despite the polls—have been willing to take a position in favor of a new treaty. The issue of compensation, discussed below, was intended to split the difference and let the Panamanian politicians eat their cake and have it too.

During the 1980s and early 1990s, the year 2000 seemed an eternity away: politicians of every persuasion could strike intransigent poses about a new treaty. This was the case as late as the Endara administration (1990–1994), which was particularly emphatic in its rejection of American bases. The vehemence of Endara and his people was perhaps understandable inasmuch as, having been installed by U.S. bayonets, they felt especially constrained to revalidate their nationalist credentials.[16] But Endara was the last Panamanian president to enjoy the luxury of being able to pass the controversy on to his successor.

Arguments against Bases. Though it rehearses some rather shopworn nationalist arguments, the Panamanian case against base retention is by no means always trivial or demagogic. To be sure, some rationales border on the metaphysical, the ideological, or the abstract. One school of thought holds that a new treaty would turn much of Panamanian history on its head, radically discounting the sacrifice of the martyrs who fought for generations to expel the Americans from the isthmus. As one of the original negotiators of the Carter-Torrijos treaties, former foreign minister Carlos López Guevara, puts it, to allow a residual U.S. military presence would "limit Panama's possibilities to develop as a nation."[17] Ruben Blades, salsa singer and founder of the Papa Egoro Party (and 1994 presidential candidate), insists that to allow the bases to remain would be tantamount to telling the world that "we are ... unable to assume the responsibilities of a free country " and would reveal Panama as "a colony disguised as a republic."[18]

Senior Panamanian diplomat Julio Linares agrees, declaring that "a nation that permanently requires foreign tutelage is destined to disappear. Nations," he adds, "must learn to stand on their feet."[19] Linares subscribes to a kind of geographical fatalism. With the best will in the world, he insists, Panama is ill situated to negotiate a satisfactory agreement with the United States, even if such were in its interests. "Only a politically and economically independent state, with sufficient moral strength, could sit down with another state as an equal partner and reach a just agreement." Since the 1989 invasion, he candidly admits, "we are highly doubtful that we have the conditions to reach such a balanced agreement with the United States." And, he adds, "it is shameful of us to beg U.S. leaders to keep their troops on our territory after the deadlines stated in the current treaties. What happened to the generational struggle waged by Panamanians and all the years of sacrifice by our youth?"[20]

Other critics of base renegotiation cite more concrete considerations. To prolong the U.S. military presence in Panama would supposedly imperil the country's fragile civilian political institutions. "If the military bases remain here partially or totally," writes *La Prensa* publisher Roberto Eisenmann, "the military gringos will again militarize our Civilian Police, making it again a Mafia of thugs, which would yield another Noriega, who would imbue himself in crazy nationalism, triggering another invasion, and bingo, we are making the same mistake over and over again!"[21] At a minimum, Fernando Manfredo asserts, "as long as we have a U.S. military presence in Panama, the U.S. permanent involvement in Panama's internal affairs is inevitable."[22]

For yet others, it is not at all clear that a residual base presence would even yield significant economic benefits to the country. Columnist Roberto N. Méndez writes that contrary to popular imaginings, the bases themselves only contribute $188 million a year to the local economy, a "much smaller [amount] than the country will receive" in the value of properties reverted in the year 2000. Moreover, Méndez argues, whatever the country loses from the bases could easily be made up from canal revenues. In 1991 he wrote that more than one-fourth of the $330 million the country received from the facility "is squandered by the Panama Canal Commission in swollen 'expenditures' benefiting U.S. military personnel and civilian bureaucrats [which] could easily be eliminated." Méndez revived an old idea—that the tolls are too low and that once in full control the Panamanian government could increase them as much as it wished with no loss of traffic or revenue, a far preferable solution to permitting American soldiers to remain.[23]

A more systematic review by the Center for Economic Research at the University of Panama arrives at broadly similar conclusions. According to its study, released in 1995, the general effect of shutting down the bases would be to deprive the Panamanian economy of about $307 million a year, less than 5 percent of the nominal value of the indicator ($469 million when the "ripple" effect is taken into account). Presumably, this would amount to no more than 2 percent of the country's gross domestic product. One of the participants in the study even advanced the notion that the value of the canal areas alone (excluding the waters, areas already reverted, and the value of the forests) amounted to $5 billion, although he did not specify how this figure could be translated into revenues without further investment.[24]

A parallel survey carried out at the same time by the Instituto de Estudios Nacionales (IDEN), an independent think tank, likewise argued that the economic contribution of the bases to Panama's welfare had been greatly exaggerated. "According to our estimates," IDEN President Juan Jovane announced, "the total expenses of military bases account for approximately 4.5 percent of Gross Domestic Product, while [their] direct and indirect impact is lower than 5 percent." Moreover, military properties already reverted to the Panamanian government or scheduled to be reverted were probably worth in the neighborhood of $30 billion balboas (dollars), "a significant part of which can be used for civilian economic purposes."[25]

The bases are also seen as a dangerous strategic liability for Panama. Some discussion on this subject is frankly lurid but is nonetheless useful for providing some sense of the texture of the debate, at least at its most ragged edges. As Roberto Méndez explains it, the bases render Panama a potential military target in the event of war, as demonstrated by the recent Persian Gulf conflict. Politician-journalist Raúl Leis goes considerably further than this: "On account of the military bases, our country is a logistics and command center of the armed forces of a superpower that controls a vital transportation link (the Canal) and a potential site to stockpile strategic (nuclear) armament."

Leis admits that he does not know whether there are nuclear weapons at American military bases in Panama, but, citing such sources as the Soviet Academy of Sciences and unnamed Western experts, he suggests that it is by no means impossible. At a minimum, Leis insists, the bases "are in condition to receive nuclear weapons," and American warships moving in and out of the area are equipped with them. "Believe it or not," he concludes, "Panama is part of the link in the strategic plans of the most powerful military nation in the world. This country is an involuntary host for all the deadly weapons that transit the Canal through some of the most populated areas of the isthmus, subject to the double risk of accidents and wars that would lead to a tragedy in our country." If, as he deems likely, atomic weapons are stationed in Panama, then the United States is violating both Carter-Torrijos treaties and the Treaty of Tlatelolco (the Latin American version of the nonproliferation treaty). At a minimum, Panama should be a country "without an internal or external army, neutral, demilitarized as relates to conflicts, without gratuitous enemies or threats." Such an eventuality is incompatible with any kind of military alliance or association with the United States.[26]

Perhaps the most original argument contends that merely raising the issue of a residual base presence is in and of itself politically destabilizing and therefore bound to bring deleterious economic consequences for the country. As an editorial writer in *La Prensa* explains (August 7, 1996), "The streets determine our reality." Once any Panamanian government sets about negotiating with the United States, "foreign investors interested in investing in Panama will again begin to flee once the flag-burning scenes of the past [once again] start to take place." "The Canal transfer we all hoped would take place imperceptibly, will turn confusing; we will undermine our costly constitutional demilitarization, and once again place the country on the verge of an unnecessary constitutional, economic and social crisis." And the newspaper concludes: "Do not frustrate our historical aspirations..., do not lead the country to a crisis that could have irreparable consequences."

Finally, the bases are seen as the source of all Panama's ills, large and small: U.S. military intervention in the country's internal affairs; an incentive to smuggling ($30 million worth annually); the entry point for "disease and vice, including AIDS and drug addiction"; and the primary cause of the country's peculiar demography, particularly as it relates to the distorted urban development of Panama City and Colón. "Instead of growing in circles or semi-circles, these cities have grown horizontally, or, in the case of Colón, by sections, which has aggravated the transportation problem and increased the price of land."[27] Presumably, the absence of the bases would right all these wrongs.

Arguments for Bases. The case for some sort of extended U.S. military presence in Panama is built on three propositions. First, the existence of American bases provides a note of reassurance to third parties, particularly the international shipping community and foreigners interested in investing in the country. The implicit assumption is that, in the presence of American troops, nothing too strange would be allowed to happen—which has certainly been the case historically. Conversely, without the Americans, the country would lose a priceless psychological asset that has kept its risk rating artificially low for eight decades. Even major personalities who are not on record as favoring a new treaty have admitted this in one way or another, notably canal administrator Gilberto Guardia;[28] former president Nicolás Ardito Barletta, who now heads the Regional Interoceanic Authority (ARI), the agency in charge of administering reverted U.S. military properties;[29] and Ricardo Roberto Arias, foreign minister under President Pérez Balladares.[30]

The second proposition is that an American military presence provides a safety net for essential public services in the event of a collapse of order in Panama itself. "What organization," asks Carlos Luis Linares Brin, "will guarantee [its] protection? The National Police could not even ensure uninterrupted traffic to and from the Colón Free Zone during the recent disturbances and trucker's strike."[31]

The third and most important point is the economic losses the country would suffer from the closing of American bases, in terms of dollars no longer spent by the soldiers and their families, combined with the costs of maintaining the facilities until they have been properly transformed into productive alternatives.[32] The principal purveyors of this line are members of the business community, leaders of unions representing civilian employees of the U.S. defense establishment, and politicians associated with the MOLIRENA and MORENA Parties.[33] Before 1994, such people were extremely circumspect in their pronouncements; in the past two or three years, they have become somewhat more voluble.

A case in point is Leo González, a member of the National Assembly for the MOLIRENA Party, who has repeatedly asserted that "it would be a crime against the fatherland to let the Americans leave Panama if we do not have any [economic] alternative."[34] Who, he asks, in the Panamanian economy could pay the work force at the canal and the bases "the $5, $6, or $7 per hour they are currently making?"[35] Another is Ray Bishop, secretary-general of Local 907, Armed Forces Employees Union (AFL-CIO), who predicts that closing the bases "will condemn 85,000 [Panamanian] families to exile or probably poverty as it has never been seen in this country. Included will be all commerce, industry, and [those] Panamanians who depend indirectly and directly on the money coming" from those installations.[36] Still another is Pedro Vallarino, president of the MORENA Party and scion of one of Panama's most important business families. According to him, for every 1,000 U.S. soldiers stationed in the country, Panama receives roughly $30,000 a year. By his calculation, some 25,000 workers could be affected. Vallarino also recites some statistics on the secondary and tertiary employment created by the U.S. presence: the U.S. military currently spends $100 million dollars each year on food, rent, and other purposes.[37]

For some, these cruel numbers have put Panamanian nationalism up at a considerable discount. "Are we going to eat the flag or the reverted land?" González pointedly asks.[38] Why indulge in "false nationalism," labor leader Mario Archer inquires, "while there is hunger and unemployment?"[39] "Nationalism," remarks Pedro Vallarino, "cannot be eaten."[40] "We do not have to stick obstinately to the mistaken idea," wrote Pérez Balladares's first foreign minister, Gabriel Lewis, "that we would not be lord and master of our territory if there were one single foreigner left."[41] If Spain, Turkey, and the Philippines could successfully negotiate base agreements with the United States "without nationalist complexes," muses Carlos Luis Linares Brin, "I do not see why Panama cannot do so."[42] And, he adds, "true nationalism should seek the country's better interests on a long-term basis and with an overall vision. It should also take into account the opinions of the people"[43] Since 1991, González and Bishop have jointly chaired a committee demanding a referendum about a U.S. base presence. Presumably with an eye to public opinion polls, they have repeatedly asserted that such an exercise would overrule once and for all the "aberrant and noisy minorities" whom, they claim, represent nobody but themselves.[44]

The Fernández-Ponce Report

The constant brandishing of facts and figures by both sides of the bases argument led the Pérez Balladares administration to commission an extensive report by Marcos Fernández and José Galán Ponce, two prominent Panamanian economists. (The former is a partner in the consulting firm of Planning Minister Guillermo Chapman.) The study was intended to resolve the question of whether the military bases served Panama best as they were being used or whether they should be converted to civilian purposes. Originally scheduled for release in February 1996, its publication was mysteriously delayed a month. According to one authoritative source, "U.S. officials and Panamanians not affiliated with the [Pérez] Balladares government speculate that the delay was political" in that some officials allegedly wanted to "manipulate the study's findings [or] in some instances, even to change them."[45] It is difficult to see what could be gained by this, since the report—valuable though it was in many respects—hardly put an end to the controversy.

Fernández-Ponce calculated that every American soldier stationed in the country represented a net contribution of $35,000 per year and that, during the first five years after definitive American withdrawal in the year 2000, Panama would suffer an annual loss of $180 million in revenue. During the second five-year period (2005–2010), the deficit would drop to $175 million and eventually bottom out at $172 million in the fifteenth year (2015).

The same study, however, affirmed that military use of Panamanian properties was not particularly beneficial and that other alternatives held out the prospect of "much higher profitability." It spoke of converting the bases into container parks, storage centers, and industrial zones, generating 4,700 jobs in the first five years (2000–2005) and up to 72,000 by the second decade of the twenty-first century. This figure is many times the number currently employed at U.S. defense sites (3,566), though the report admitted that those same workers took home three-and-a-half times the average salary paid elsewhere in Panama.

Further, Fernández-Ponce frankly conceded that Howard Air Force Base and Fort Sherman did not present any "very short term" economic use, both because they were not necessary for the harmonious development of the rest of the country and because they would have high maintenance costs. The report therefore suggested that these two bases be jointly shared by Panama and the United States, with the latter paying the former some sort of compensation. If base rent were not obtainable, then the government should seek some sort of preferential commercial arrangement from Washington (either trade concessions, such as Panamanian accession to NAFTA, investment guarantee mechanisms, or support for tourism and other forms of private investment). Panama should also ask the United States to construct two bridges and a road to connect Fort Sherman to Colón and Costa Abajo.[46]

Like many government or government-commissioned documents, the Ponce-Fernández report had something for everybody. It substantiated the high costs of American withdrawal in the short run, without subscribing to the notion that Panama was helpless to do anything about it. It provided a series of optimistic projections about the nonmilitary use of American base properties that were plausible though not inevitable. (They were based on the perhaps gratuitous assumption that the country would inspire sufficient confidence without an American presence to attract significant amounts of foreign investment and also that Panama's educational and administrative institutions would prove equal to the demands of the high-tech age. Additionally, the study took as a given that a tradition in Panama of using public wealth for private gain would be extinct, at least by the year 2020.) Probably, its principal contribution was to legitimize the notion that some American bases might remain in Panama provided the United States offered a handsome compensation package in return.

The Moment of Truth for the Bases Issue

Before release of the Ponce-Fernández report, the notion that the permanence of some U.S. bases might be in the Panamanian national interest was regarded as beyond the pale of political respectability. The only major figure willing to advocate this solution publicly was Rubén Darío Carlés, who ran on the MOLIRENA ticket in the 1994 presidential election. An austere, somewhat dyspeptic economist who had served as the comptroller-general of the Endara administration, Carlés was not one to mince words. When the subject was raised in a radio debate, he snapped that it was time to "stop talking nonsense." Under the neutrality treaty, the United States had obtained the right "to intervene and return to Panama whenever it feels there is a justified reason, which it can easily interpret in its own way." If Panamanians regretted this state of affairs, they should blame Omar Torrijos, "who placed us under the Pentagon's umbrella." Whether the United States possessed bases in the country was really quite irrelevant. But since the Americans obviously wanted to remain, Panama should make the best of a bad bargain and use the bases to leverage a preferential trade agreement.[47]

During the campaign, Pérez Balladares, like all the other major candidates, wholly rejected the idea. Once elected, however, he sounded an entirely new note. While frankly avowing that he could see no "geopolitical reason" for the bases to remain, "if there is any other reason for a small and medium-sized U.S. military presence in Panama the United States would have to say what it is and propose it to the Panamanians. Then we would have to look at our national interests, strictly from a security and military viewpoint." He categorically denied that "the positive or negative [economic] consequences" could form the basis of a decision by the Panamanian government, which in any case would have to be submitted to a plebiscite.[48]

These remarks marked the beginning of a complicated ballet between the two governments, in which each defied the other to jump in the water first. The United States was reluctant to raise the issue at all for fear of being seen as in violation of the spirit (if not precisely the letter) of Carter-Torrijos; the Panamanian government felt itself unable to initiate discussion, both because this would place it in a disadvantageous bargaining position and because of the perception within Panama that the question amounted to a diplomatic and political hot potato. The humiliating spectacle of begging the United States to remain—after so many decades of asking it to leave, public opinion polls be damned—was not lost on the Panamanian political class, either.[49]

Finally, on September 6, 1995, the ice was broken in a joint agreement announced on the occasion of a state visit to Washington of President Pérez Balladares. Both countries committed themselves to begin informal discussions to determine if there was a mutual interest in the United States maintaining a military presence in Panama beyond the year 1999. In November 1996, fourteen months later, however, the Panamanian president suddenly ended the possibility by announcing to a meeting of the youth wing of his own party that there would be no U.S. forces in the country after the year 2000. What happened during the intervening period casts a revealing light on the dynamics of both Panamanian politics and U.S.-Panamanian relations.

During the early months of this period, discussions between Foreign Minister Gabriel Lewis and U.S. Ambassador William Hughes and SouthCom Commander General Barry McCaffrey apparently led to an informal understanding that would have permitted a residual base presence, at least in principle. In one presumably authoritative version, the U.S. military would be allowed to keep Howard Air Force Base, Rodman Naval Station, Fort Kobbe, and Galeta Island, with the fate of

Fort Sherman, Fort Clayton, and Corozal left to subsequent negotiations.[50]

But it soon became clear that the Pérez Balladares administration would go forward with the project only if it received sufficient political cover in the form of a major economic compensation package from the United States, as either base rent or other incentives outlined in the Fernández-Ponce report. Since the United States was not prepared to offer any of these concessions, the negotiation effectively came to an end. "As long as the [U.S.] position that there will be no economic compensation for Panama prevails," Pérez Balladares told the press, "I do not foresee a resumption [of talks] in the immediate future."[51] Lewis resigned because of ill health in May 1996 and died the following December. He was replaced by the Panamanian ambassador to Washington, Ricardo Roberto Arias, reputed to be far cooler to the idea of a residual U.S. military presence.

Obstacles to Compensation. The compensation issue was the fundamental sticking point. From the Panamanian point of view, the question could not have arisen at a less opportune moment, when the end of the cold war mandated significant reductions in the U.S. defense budget. Among other things, this led to the closing of U.S. bases around the world and, to even greater political effect, in many parts of the continental United States. Why any member of Congress would vote to keep a Panamanian base open while closing one in his home district taxes the political imagination; in the particular case of Panama, to duplicate the obvious economic benefits of a base presence by providing an additional sweetener exceeds all logical possibility.

As far as the United States is concerned, the practice of paying rent for overseas military bases—in itself unusual—has not existed for decades. Far from paying Germany and Japan for the privilege of stationing troops on their territory, these countries actually compensate the United States for providing for their defense. (When told of this, Panamanian politicians typically dismiss the matter by arguing that "after all, they lost the war.") One serviceable example would seem to be the U.S.-Spanish Friendship Treaty of 1976: the United States compensated Spain for the use of base facilities in the amount of approximately $1 billion, largely to finance military equipment, air defense facilities, and specialized training. But no such agreement has been reached with any country since the end of the cold war, and, barring a radical shift in the geopolitical situation worldwide, none is likely.

The one exception within the region—the U.S. naval facility at Guantánamo Bay in Cuba—is an anomaly from the early years of this century. The payment for use of this base amounts only to a few thousand dollars a month. As a sign of his refusal to recognize the right to a U.S. presence there, dictator Fidel Castro has not signed any of the checks for more than thirty-five years.

Finally, it is difficult to see why the United States should pile additional incentives on top of the already $250 million–300 million that the Panamanian economy receives from the American military presence, not to mention the intangible benefits provided by the troops in risk insurance to foreign investors, unless one believes that there is something uniquely—indeed, supremely—valuable about Panamanian geography. Evidently, key figures in the U.S. military, naval, and diplomatic establishment in Panama do believe this, and their views appear to be shared by some defense intellectuals in Washington. So do some members of the U.S. Congress. So far, none of these groups, however, has succeeded in advancing its point of view—complete with its yet undefined price tag—either at the White House or on Capitol Hill. [52]

Political Conflict. If the Pérez Balladares administration has seemed notably maladroit in the way it has managed the entire subject of a residual American presence, this is largely because it has been fighting a two-front war. On one side is Washington, increasingly driven by post–cold war budgetary constraints; on the other, the broad range of opposition parties within Panama, collectively determined to raise the threshold of an acceptable agreement. By introducing the notion of base rent (or some other form of compensation) in the first place, Pérez Balladares not only kindled public expectations but mortgaged his own political credibility to a doubtful proposition; namely, the United States would be willing to pay for the privilege of remaining in Panama. When this proved not to be the case, the president's critics at home were left free to say that they would have disapproved of a residual base presence under any circumstances.

Even if the United States had been willing to offer a compensation package, however, it is worth speculating whether President Pérez Balladares would have been able to deliver on an agreement. On this subject his own party has been deeply divided, as has (reportedly) his own cabinet.[53] As recently as January 1997, for example, PRD President Gerardo González reaffirmed that "there will be no [American] bases in Panama's future, while ritually the same day the president of the Legislative Assembly, César Pardo, suggested that there could be talks on the subject sometime *after* December 31, 1999, "should the Need arise."[54]

For its part, throughout 1996 the major opposition parties—MOLIRENA, the Arnulfistas, and the Christian Democrats—played a cynical cat-and-mouse-game with the government on the subject of the bases; they claimed that they could not articulate a position until the government had actually approached them with a proposal. (Even when Minister Arias met with the leadership of the individual parties, this session was interpreted by the latter as a photo opportunity rather than a substantive consultation.[55] Of all the politicians interviewed by a staff delegation from the U.S. Senate in late 1996, only two Christian Democrats, former vice-president Ricardo Arias Calderon and party president Ruben Arosemena, were willing to admit flatly that they would oppose a base extension on grounds on principle.[56] Other leaders of the opposition preferred to cut Pérez Balladares just enough slack to hang himself.

The Multilateral Counterdrug Center. Once it was established that the Clinton administration rejected the idea of bases in exchange for economic compensation, Lewis and Pérez Balladares devised a new proposal: the creation of a multilateral counterdrug center (MCC) using Howard Air Force Base. This plan would permit some American troops to remain in Panama for narcotics interdiction. The center itself would be run by civilians and would be multilateral, in the sense that it would provide berths for representatives from a number of Latin American countries. The Panamanian government has said that no economic compensation package would be required from the United States to justify the center, though one Panamanian official told a Senate staffer earlier in 1997 that the United States, along with other countries, "would have to make proportionate operational payments for use" of the facility.[57]

The MCC concept was controversial from the start. In the first place, most Latin American nations are not particularly anxious to enlist their armed forces in the fight against drugs. Thus, when Panama proposed the creation of the center at the defense ministerial of the Miami summit held in Bariloche, Argentina, in October 1996, the response ran from tepid to hostile. Additionally, the Rio Group, the largest diplomatic coalition of Latin American nations, has flatly rejected the idea. The lack of Latin American support is particularly troubling to Panamanians since without it their country would be unnecessarily exposed "to international political risks ... drag [ged] ... into potentially damaging controversies with our neighbors." [58]

Second, many in the United States feel that what Panama is proposing is already largely in place at Howard to the extent that the U.S. military there is engaged in counternarcotics intelligence and operations, complete with a complement of civilians drawn from U.S. Customs, the U.S. Coast Guard, and the Drug Enforcement Agency. Permanent complements of foreign military advisers, mostly from other Latin American countries, are also stationed there. Under the Panamanian proposal, these activities would no longer be subject to U.S. operational control, a change that would presumably compromise communications security and other military essentials.

Third, the U.S. military interest in Panama extends beyond Howard and counternarcotics activities. The U.S. Southern Command would like to keep or have access to seven facilities to continue its humanitarian, civic action, and training missions in or from Panama. This access runs counter to the frequently articulated position of the Panamanian government that the MCC is not a cover for a continued U.S. military presence. A similar difference of opinion has divided the two governments on troop sizes. The Panamanian government has long stated that it wants no more than 400–500 American military people at the center, while SouthCom has consistently thought in terms of several thousand. [59] Not surprisingly, then, the process of negotiation has been long and tortuous.

Despite widespread pessimism, both governments announced that a preliminary agreement had been reached Christmas Eve 1997. [60] Although many details have yet to be ironed out, its main lines are as follows. [61] Approximately 1,500–2,000 personnel will be assigned to the center; roughly 80 percent will be U.S. military and civilian personnel. The largest complement (about two-thirds) will come from the air force; approximately one-quarter will be drawn from the U.S. Army; and a tiny complement of navy personnel will run the Small Craft Instruction and Training School. There will also be a small detachment from the U.S. Special Forces.

The "multilaterality" will presumably be satisfied by a handful of personnel from other Latin American countries. President Pérez Balladares believes that this condition will be satisfied when at least two other countries join Panama and the United States, but neither he nor the United States is thinking of Guatemala or El Salvador. Rather, both parties are looking for contributions from major regional powers;

those most frequently mentioned are Argentina, Brazil, Peru, and Colombia (though Pérez Balladares likes to suggest Mexico). Even this is not quite what it seems. There would be little or no real military representation; most personnel dispatched from these countries would be officers and men from the national police or drug enforcement agencies (and in the case of Mexico, even this is doubtful). Even Argentina, whose current defense policy calls for active alignment with the United States in world affairs, may be unable to participate in the full sense since its constitution prohibits involvement of the military in police operations except to provide logistical support to constabulary-type forces.[62] If the opposition Radical-FREPASO coalition wins the 1999 presidential elections in that country, however, even that modest contribution may end since that political community has long advocated an end to Argentine military participation of any kind in the drug war.

Even if a credible coalition could be cobbled together, other obstacles lay ahead. In the first place, the U.S. Senate is likely to wish to scrutinize the agreement since it would, in theory at least, require a new treaty. No doubt the Clinton administration would prefer to bypass the ratification process through an executive agreement, but that would contravene Article 5 of the neutrality treaty, which states unambiguously that "after the termination of the Panama Canal Treaty, only the Republic of Panama shall ... maintain military forces, defense sites, and military installations within its national territory." (Of course, nothing in either of the canal treaties precludes the conclusion of a successor document.)

But with whom would Washington conclude such an instrument? So far neither the United Nations nor the Organization of American States nor any other collective international actor has offered to loan the center its flag; the best that President Pérez Balladares can lamely offer is a committee of foreign ministers of participating countries, headed by his own, to supervise the activities of the center. [63] As far as the United States is concerned, this begs crucial questions of command, control, and the safety of American personnel and their families. [64]

Moreover, the proposal must be passed by a vote of the Panamanian Legislative Assembly and then ratified by the public by plebiscite. At one time, this would have been a mere formality. As noted in chapter 3, as late as 1995 all polls reflected a persistent willingness to contemplate a U.S. base presence in the country beyond the year 2000 without apparent conditions. Once the issue of compensation was introduced into the discussion, however, the public reframed the issue.

Approval became conditional on the assurance of additional economic benefits. This turnaround is evident in a survey carried out in December 1996: 81 percent favored allowing some American bases to remain provided compensation was paid; in the event that the United States persisted in refusing a benefits package, however, 64 percent were opposed. (Even so, fully 72 percent favored a return to the negotiating table.) Three months later, 70 percent favored the creation of the multilateral counternarcotics center, presumably because it represented a new and more effective ploy to extract dollars from Washington. [65]

Unfortunately, except for a peppercorn rent for a few buildings, no such compensation is offered in the current proposal. Under such circumstances, the opposition parties, which together represent the overwhelming majority of organized opinion, can be expected to make the most of the fact. Beyond the matter of cash, some opposition leaders seriously question whether the center would serve its ostensible purpose. "What is the use," Gloria Young, president of the Papa Egoro Party, asked, "of having military bases to fight drug trafficking if the United States is the largest consumer of cocaine and other drugs even though it has the largest military forces and the largest economic power worldwide?"[66] This is a logic that appeals even to some members of the president's own party. PRD legislator Víctor López recommended that the United States "clean up its own house insted of worrying about military bases on Panamanian territory."[67]

Quite apart from economic considerations, the plebiscite may fail by being overloaded with other cargo. Specifically, for some time now, the Democratic Revolutionary Party has been trying to figure out a way to change the Constitution to permit consecutive presidential terms; under such circumstances, Pérez Balladares would be eligible to run for reelection in 1999. If the ballot contains a provision dealing with this subject, the opposition parties can be expected to redouble their efforts to achieve a "no" vote.

Questions Worth Pondering

If the United States had been unwilling to consider a compensation package for Panama from the beginning, it is difficult to see how any kind of agreement on base retention could have been achieved. Whether the same fate befalls the multilateral counternarcotics center remains to be seen. Even so, several questions remain for the United States. If military facilities in Panama were so vital to the U.S. military presence in the Western Hemisphere, why were they so readily surrendered in the Carter-Torrijos treaties? Presumably, the U.S. negotiators, armed with public opinion polls and private assurances from Panamanian business and political leaders, assumed that by the time the year 2000 rolled around, the Panamanian people would have a change of heart.[68] On the evidence, they have proved wrong. While Panamanians as a whole believe that the bases benefit their country, they have been led to think that they benefit the United States more; therefore, the latter should provide additional compensation for their presence. If this opinion holds firm, the Pérez Balladares administration will lose the plebiscite.

While the multinational counternarcotics center clearly addresses some of the newer security concerns of the United States in the circum-Caribbean reign, as defined by Panama it falls short of the minimal needs of the Southern Command. The difference between 400–500 army troops, for example, and several thousand is both qualitative and quantitative. While there is some evidence that the original proposal as crafted by Minister Lewis was intended to be an entering wedge for something more, the response to the idea by the political opposition in Panama has thrown the Pérez Balladares administration onto the defensive. Its actions cannot validate what its opponents accuse it of doing.

Insofar as the United States is concerned, it is far from clear that the multilateral counternarcotics center will be of much benefit at all. Or, whatever benefit might be forthcoming will be counterbalanced by other considerations. Whether the United States stations 500 or 5,000 troops in Panama makes a great deal of difference in terms of the strategic weight of its presence and the particular kinds and number of missions that it can accomplish but none whatever in terms of its political exposure. Even with a complement of only 500 troops—or, if one adds in the air force component and the tiny navy detachment, roughly 1,500—the United States will still be held responsible for Panama's welfare and blamed for all its shortcomings. A small garrison would carry with it all the political liabilities of a neocolonial situation with few of its benefits.

Any U.S. military community in Panama, whether large or small, is perennially hostage to the vagaries of local political conditions. But when it is small, it is especially vulnerable. In the past, the sheer enormity of the American presence was a stabilizing factor in Panamanian politics and a deterrent to violence against its resident nationals. Five hundred, 1,000, even 1,500 troops would possess minimal deterrence value and would probably be irrelevant to Panamanian stability. But the military presence would act as a tripwire for U.S. intervention. After all, attacks on U.S. civilians, not threats to the canal, led to the American invasion of 1989.

Of course, for those in Panama who favor it, the presence of American troops, no matter how small the number, is the name of the game. In this sense, the multilaterality of the drug center, regardless of how patently bogus, is a fig leaf that allows the country both to claim its independence and to shelter behind U.S. power. Unfortunately, the drug center is a preposterously weak reed on which to lean. It would have nothing whatever to do with factors affecting Panama's success or failure as a nation. The center would not affect the administration of the canal, for good or for ill. It would contribute nothing to the management of the environment. It would not replace the Panamanian army or play a role in securing Panama's southern border against drug traffickers. It would not even be in a position to act effectively in cases of civil disorder since the infantry and military police components would be minimal or nonexistent. Even the direct economic benefits of the center would be minimal since it would consist of only 2,000 people, many of them on hardship tours and therefore unaccompanied by their families.

The heart of the revisionist issue is not, in fact, so much about dollars as it is about the fear that many, perhaps most, Panamanians have—for all their vituperative rhetoric against the United States—of standing alone in the world. As one Senate staff report points out with remarkable insight, the negotiations over a residual base presence were only coincidentally about military installations. "Panama," it concluded, "wants a strategic relationship with the United States. [It] wants something that goes beyond a continued U.S. military presence."[69] For many years, this relationship was demonstrated in two ways. One was the common boundary between Panama and the United States shared on both sides of the zone; the other was the physical presence of a huge American military community. This situation gave Panama a special place in the universe of American foreign and security policy and assured it of far greater attention in Washington than other Central American or Caribbean countries. From a geopolitical point of view, Panama weighed in more like Venezuela or Colombia than Costa Rica; in terms of regional priorities, perhaps only Mexico and Cuba—for very different reasons—occupied a more important place in the American scheme of things.

Like the Philippines, which until recently shared some important similarities, Panama never had to go to the international lending institutions alone, never had to worry about getting its phone calls to Washington answered, never had to contemplate the possibility of falling out of bed politically or economically. The Carter-Torrijos treaties set into motion a process that, whether Panamanians themselves were conscious or it or not, reduced their country's relative importance. Apparently, the Panamanian negotiators of the treaties imagined that they could abandon the special military relationship with the United States without diminishing their country's strategic weight. By the time the facts of the case dawned on the country's leadership class, it was already too late. The cold war had ended, and the process of devolution—not just of the canal but of the bases—was already far advanced.

The outcome may be a positive one, nonetheless. It all depends on how the country manages the assets received from the United States and the degree to which it can transform itself from an American strategic enclave into an ordinary Latin American country. A brief survey of these prospects would seem to be the proper place to conclude.

6

---------------- ✦ ----------------

Toward the Year 2000 and After

Behind the debate over a residual U.S. military presence in Panama lurks an unpleasant fact—namely, that since the ratification of the Carter-Torrijos treaties, successive Panamanian governments have conspicuously failed to make productive use of the resources that were expected to compensate for the economic benefits of American bases.

The Reverted Areas

These properties, known collectively as the reverted areas, take in 364,078 acres of land and 7,000 buildings and facilities. Roughly two-thirds of this territory consists of unimproved lands belonging to the old Panama Canal Zone. But the other third consists of military bases, administrative facilities, and a large firing range and munitions depot operated by the U.S. military. Since 1979, only about 1,300 buildings have been turned over to Panama; in slightly more than two years, the country must find a use for a huge amount of real estate, much of it in or near urban areas. By one calculation, the total value of the military installations themselves exceeds $2.9 billion, and the reverted assets in their totality approach $5 billion.[1]

Just why both governments proceeded with the transfer at such a leisurely pace is difficult to say. The United States probably held the lingering expectation that as the year 2000 approached, the Panamanians would come around to offering to lease back some of the more essential properties. The Panamanians may merely have been reluctant to contemplate their conversion to civilian use—a plausible theory given that from the ratification of Carter-Torrijos in 1977 to the U.S. invasion in 1989, the country labored under military or military-dominated governments.[2]

Whatever the reason, for a decade and a half only marginal properties were transferred to the Panamanian authorities. Even so, the consequences did not escape public notice. The most notable failure was, as noted, the Panama Railroad, which once ferried cargo and passengers across the isthmus. Surrendered immediately after ratification, today the rolling stock lies in ruins, and grass grows between its rotting rails. Another example—and one that cannot be explained away by military rule since the facility was handed over to the Endara government in 1991—is the Coco Solo military base. Located on the Atlantic side of the canal, this was once an attractive complex of administrative buildings and barracks, rendered in the traditional zonian architectural style. In the words of one journalist, "it began to rot almost as soon as the air conditioning was turned off. Before long, looters had stripped the buildings of even plumbing and wiring. Today, Coco Solo is an overgrown squatter's camp."[3]

The collapse of the Panama Railroad was due to politics as usual in the country's public sector, namely, padding payrolls with unnecessary employees and hiring expensive "consultants" with good political connections. But the dramatic decline of Coco Solo, which even President Pérez Balladares called a "national disgrace,"[4] was due to a lack of maintenance and to an inattention to security. Concretely, Panama's eight-month rainy season exposes many areas to as much as 200 inches of rainfall: "Anything that is not protected by constant polish and sweat is soon claimed by the jungle."[5] To be sure, Coco Solo could hardly be adequately guarded as long as officials were complaining that the country lacked adequate forces to police the canal itself.[6]

If Panama cannot convert U.S. military properties to immediate commercial use, then they must be mothballed until someone is found to activate their economic potential. If they are to be maintained and protected while awaiting eventual conversion, far from representing a net gain to the country they threaten to impose charges of anywhere from $30 million–40 million a year. The Fernández-Ponce report underscored this problem by predicting that fully twenty-five years after reversion only one-third of the properties would be fully utilized.[7] These considerations explain why in recent years the government of Panama has been requesting the United States to delay actual transfer of certain properties[8] and also accounts for the effort to extract additional benefits from Washington in exchange for a residual base presence.

The uninspiring record of administration of reverted areas under the military (and, to some extent, under Endara) has dealt a stunning blow to Panamanian self-confidence. "Now that we are very close to assuming full jurisdiction over our entire territory," Gabriel Lewis wrote, "we are afraid.... Some think that Panama is finished if the Americans leave for good."[9] "We have failed to put the reverted areas to good use, and we are not ready to receive what is about to revert," Christian Democratic leader Guillermo Cóchez declared. "We have failed to draw up an economic development program for those areas which will compensate for the jobs that will disappear with the closing ... of the military bases."[10] Television correspondent Fernando Fam noted, "The example we set so far with the property that has been reverted is a national shame. Whether we like it or not, we have demonstrated that the constant cries of dignity and sovereignty are but a romantic dream that keeps us far from world reality."[11]

One Panamanian journalist cites examples, chapter and verse: "Garbage collection services were returned to us and we went from being one of the cleanest cities in Latin America" to one of the most unsanitary. "We were given the task of purifying water and now we are buying what we at one time got for free. We received a railroad system that was a model of efficiency and we have turned it into a junkyard. We were given an international airport with all its equipment and we have turned it into a stable." While this was happening, the government was spending $10 million to repair and refurbish the Paitilla Airport, "which should have been closed and transferred to Albrook.... We received housing and gardens that were the envy of Bella Vista and Altos del Golf[12] residents and we have turned them into slums and private dumps."[13]

The experience of the reverted areas has even raised questions about Panama's ultimate capacity to administer the canal itself. As editorial writer Rafael Mezquita put it last year, the transfer of that facility to a Panamanian administration "will be traumatic.... Its market continues to decrease in relative terms.... Its personnel will experience the difference between working with the dominating, organization culture of a powerful country, the U.S., and starting a new relation with the dependent culture of a weak country, Panama." He continued:

As a result of our play-it-smart culture, which is practiced by both the people and the government, people "avoid" paying their bills to government institutions. It has happened with the ports and the railroad. It could happen with the Canal. Regardless of the political will ... and the resources ... invested in the transition, when the Canal passes to Panamanian administration, a new system will be established that could be characterized by a relaxation of discipline, respect for regulations, and even the fear that existed in the previous administration.[14]

The Regional Interoceanic Authority

These doubts were apparently shared by the general public. A poll conducted in the spring of 1992 revealed that fully 70 percent of Panamanians did not believe that their government was ready to administer the canal on its own, and 92 percent responded that the reverted areas were not being properly used.[15] By way of response, in February 1993 President Endara created the Regional Interoceanic Authority (ARI) to guard, use, and administer reverted properties and named as its director Carlos Mendoza, respected publisher of the important daily *El Panamá-América*. Shortly after his inauguration, President Pérez Balladares replaced Mendoza with José Chen Barria, but a controversy over some changes to its charter—which led to protests by opposition members of the National Assembly and even by other ARI board members that the new administration was trying to compromise its autonomy and independence—led to Chen's resignation. In his place, Pérez Balladares named former president Nicolás Ardito Barletta.

Barletta immediately embarked on an international tour to sell the notion that the reverted areas represented an exceptional opportunity for foreign investors. According to the glossy publication that he carried with him, Panama's development would be based on "maritime services (privatization of ports, industrial and trade free zones, ship refueling, servicing, maintenance and repairs, container ports, cargo redistribution center), industrial parks, tourism and ecotourism, and the City of Knowledge (education, training and research centers)."[16]

Barletta fleshed out these concepts with considerable grandiosity. For Fort Amador on the Pacific side, the ARI contemplated the construction of three hotels, a shopping center, and a cruise ship terminal. Nearby Albrook Air Force Base would undergo a similar transformation, with the additional conversion of military housing into condominiums for U.S. retirees. In Corozal, west of the Gaillard Highway, installations would be established "to store dry and perishable goods, to repair vehicles," and to engage in "activities relating to warehouses and transportation." Such facilities would have access to the southern entrance of the canal before the Miraflores Locks, and although they do not presently possess adequate docking, "experts claim it is feasible for them to handle medium-sized vessels for the transshipment of merchandise."

The most important urban real estate in ARI's prospective portfolio is a complex consisting of Howard Air Force Base, Fort Kobbe, and Rodman Naval Station (known to the U.S. military as HOKORO), as well as Fort Clayton, opposite the canal. All these installations are basically part of Panama City itself, and some experts think that Clayton and Albrook will become its new downtown, given that together they possess nearly 1,800 homes, as well as a complex of schools and other amenities. Rodman's port facilities are presently usable but would have to be modified once construction begins on a third set of locks in the year 2005.

On the Atlantic side, the principal properties are Forts Davis, Espinar, and Sherman, as well as Galeta Island. Barletta touted Davis as an ideal export-processing zone, while at Espinar he contemplated the construction of a hotel at the former School of the Americas, establishment of a Swiss hotel school, construction of a commercial area, and the sale of homes to the public. Fort Sherman, former home of the jungle training school, would presumably become a center of ecotourism; it is difficult to see what else it could be, since it consists of a clearing in the jungle, beaches, largely dormitory-type housing, and a landing strip suitable only for small passenger and cargo planes. Galeta Island—whatever its utility to the U.S. Department of Defense—offers no immediate prospects for civilian use.[17]

Some Panamanians have expressed modest skepticism about these plans. One in particular who cannot be ignored is economist Marcos Fernández, coauthor of the Fernández-Ponce report. In his view, the government must be prepared to sell the properties of Amador, Albrook, and Corozal the moment they are returned, since they lie well within the urban perimeter of Panama City. Conversion of Howard Air Force Base will take place more slowly, he warned, because it has no immediate civilian use.[18] Those who imagine that Fort Sherman could become a cash cow on the order of the ecotourist centers of neighboring Costa Rica should bear in mind the perils of "land squatters who are advancing in the Costa Abajo area" and who could well despoil the territory before the tourist facilities are fully in place.

Unlike Barletta, Fernández cannot easily see an immediate use for much of the land that is to be reverted. The Americans, he wrote, "are going to return 17,000 hectares (44,000 acres) of prime land between the Pacific and the Caribbean, but 10,000 of them (26,000 acres)—roughly the size of Panama City without San Miguelito—cannot be used at all, because they are rifle ranges." Rather than fantasize about bonanzas that are unlikely to materialize, he told a meeting of the Rotary Club, "those of us who can see beyond our noses [should] understand that by the end of this century and the beginning of the next, the debate should be centered on how to maintain the standard of living we enjoy today because of the easy dollar." [19]

Reversion Blues

A 1996 staff report produced for the U.S. Senate Foreign Relations Committee provides additional underpinning to Fernández's remarks. Fort Amador, the first major installation on the Pacific side to be reverted to the Panamanian government, was supposed to be transferred on the first day of 1996. Since the government had no immediate purpose for it (Barletta's shopping malls and cruise ship ports having not yet materialized)[20] and did not relish expending the money to maintain it in a mothballed status, however, Panama asked for a delay. The best Washington could do was to postpone the reversion for nine months— to September 30—the last day for which the U.S. fiscal 1996 military budget authorized money for its operation and upkeep.

A similar situation prevailed with Forts Davis and Espinar on the Atlantic side. Seeking to avoid the $250,000 monthly maintenance costs, the Panamanian government sued for a delay in transfer. The United States refused, and the properties reverted on schedule. U.S. military officials now claim, however, that Panama has fallen behind in making payments to the American firm contracted to maintain the lawns and buildings of both facilities. Barletta told Senate staffers that by May 1997 Davis would be fully privatized, with 260 acres transformed into an industrial park by Taiwanese investors. (He also cited interest by a number of other parties.) U.S. officials in Panama expressed some doubts about this.

To date, Fort Espinar has remained largely undeveloped for civilian use. Most of its buildings, including the former School of the Americas, are deteriorating from lack of maintenance. Some buildings had reverted to the old Panama Defense Forces before 1989 and were damaged during the U.S. invasion, but no attempt has been made to restore or refurbish them. Despite the talk of a Swiss tourism and hotel management school, no contracts have been signed to date.[21] The ARI is trying to sell the housing units, with unclear success. No financing has been found to convert Albrook Air Force Base and Fort Clayton into a "City of Knowledge" or, for that matter, to convert some of the housing units at the former into retirement residences for Americans. This somber record led the Senate staff report to ask "if Panama cannot handle the buildings it has already received (1,300), how will it be able to turn over into commercial use 3,000 buildings it will receive in the next three years?"[22]

A large part of the problem is that some properties do not lend themselves to instant conversion. A case in point is Fort Amador, which cannot be used as a tourist center until it has received millions of dollars' worth of improvements: a cleanup of Panama Bay and the construction of major thoroughfares, aqueducts, and electrical power grids, as well as the installation of a world-class telephone system. In their absence, foreign investors are understandably cautious. Robert Baker, president of the American Chamber of Commerce in Panama, recently told the press that he would not consider investing in Amador "until such time as the rules of the game are clearly stipulated and businessmen are provided with adequate infrastructure."[23]

The Philippine Analogy

Panama's unimpressive record of reconversion of U.S. military facilities does not inevitably condemn it to failure. An instructive counterexample is the Philippines, another country that has long enjoyed a close and even psychologically and culturally suffocating relationship with the United States. Like the old Panama Canal Zone, the islands were annexed as a protectorate during the heyday of U.S. imperial expansion. Two American installations there, Clark Air Force Base and Subic Bay Naval Station, were for decades the axis of U.S. military power in Asia. Like Panama, too, Filipino nationalism was inevitably anti-American, though also largely a phenomenon restricted to the country's intellectual and political elite. The Philippines resembles Panama to the extent that its political history has been extremely problematic, shot through with corruption and nepotism. (There are, of course, some differences: politics in Panama has been far less violent, and most rulers of the Philippines have been civilians, not military men.)

Both countries are strategically located at the center of crucial geographical areas; both have large, well-educated, English-speaking populations; both offer a comfortable lifestyle for expatriates at a reasonable cost—"excellent housing, schools of a high standard where lessons are taught in English, modern hospitals and health care services, and varied recreational facilities."[24] For many years, the Philippines received large payments for the use of the two bases, but when the base treaty came up for renewal in the late 1980s, the United States refused to meet its price: $1 billion a year. After an exceptionally acrimonious debate, the Filipino Senate voted 12–11 to refuse extension on the lease of Subic Bay. As with Panama, this meant definitive U.S. withdrawal. The last American forces left the country in November 1992.[25]

That same year, the Philippines registered *zero* percent economic growth. This was consonant with a long period of economic stagnation, during which the country's dynamic neighbors often referred to it as the sick man of Asia. Since then, however, the Philippines has emerged as one of the Asian tigers, achieving nearly 3 percent growth in 1993 and nearly 6 percent in 1995. Unemployment is at a seventeen-year low. The key to this spectacular growth is the successful conversion of Subic Bay and Clark Air Force Base to civilian use. The latter is slated to become the future international airport for Greater Manila. Subic, formerly the biggest U.S. naval base in Asia, is now the regional hub for Federal Express, and its fueling stations are owned by the Coastal Corporation of Houston, which uses them to supply petroleum throughout the area and refuel ships plying the China Sea.

When the United States left Subic in 1992, some 42,000 Filipinos lost their jobs, and the surrounding economy was deprived of hundreds of millions of dollars in U.S. public and private disbursements. Today, those jobs have more than been replaced by new foreign investment—running at an incredible 3,000 percent a year since 1993. Behind this phenomenal record is a decision by President Fidel Ramos to reform the Filipino economy: dismantling cartels and monopolies; deregulating telecommunications, transport, insurance, and other sectors; privatizing steel, fertilizer, and shipping; liberalizing foreign investment laws; and creating an independent monetary authority. By privatizing the government electrical company and allowing foreigners to invest in energy, the country no longer suffers from crippling brown-outs. Instead, it has become an electronics subcontractor, supplying parts of microchips to Texas Instruments, Motorola, Intel, and other clients.[26]

There is no inherent reason why Panama cannot do something like this, but leadership and a drastic transformation of its political culture will be required. Panamanians still believe that their government—if not precisely the United States—owes them a living. Since his election in 1994, President Pérez Balladares has repeatedly complained that people think his government is an "employment agency."[27] "Jobs cannot be created by simply decreeing them or by simply enacting a law," he told a television interviewer. "I can't believe that anyone could think that my government, or any other government, can hire the entire population and put it on the state payroll."[28]

Perhaps no one in Panama would state the matter quite so baldly, but the available evidence would not provide much comfort for the president or any potential successors. According to a poll conducted at the end of 1996, Panamanians reject by decisive majorities the concept of privatizing the Institute of Hydraulic Resources and Electrification (78 percent), the National Waterworks and Sewer Systems Institute (76 percent), and the National Institute of Telecommunications (75 percent).[29] Consequently, even those Panamanian politicians who agree in principle that there is a need to reduce the size of the state are unwilling to face the consequences. Then-Vice-President Guillermo Ford, for example, told a television panel discussion show in 1990 that Panama's "totally paternalistic state economy needs to be changed" but denied plans for massive dismissals of public employees, as well as rumors of tax increases or price hikes.[30]

For his part, President Pérez Balladares seems amply aware of the problems that Panama's "totally paternalistic" tradition poses for the country's free integration into the world economy. During his first three years in office, he has sponsored labor, educational, and tariff reforms, while facing down considerable criticism within his own party and from opponents. He has privatized the ports of Cristóbal on the Caribbean and Balboa on the Pacific Coast. A container-hauling rail line between Cristóbal and Balboa, which has also been privatized, will be rebuilt by Kansas City Southern Industries, a subsidiary of an American carrier. In addition, a container port has operated as a joint U.S.-Panama enterprise on the Caribbean side since 1994.[31] These are excellent steps, but only the beginning of what needs to be done. Whether Panama replicates the success of the Philippines will depend in large measure on the degree to which Pérez Balladares's reforms are implemented and sustained by his successor.

The Challenge of Privatization

Given maintenance costs, Panama has no choice but to put up most reverted areas for sale to the highest bidder. This process—which one Panamanian official calls "the biggest real estate operation of the century"[32]—has invariably raised a few eyebrows. "The shenanigans are already bubbling about," one diplomat is quoted as saying. "There is that ethos here, and we keep hearing talk about payoffs and sweetheart deals and maneuvering and infighting to see who gets what."[33] In and of itself this is nothing new, though in the context of the U.S. withdrawal the situation may have a deleterious effect on the country's stability, since new resources must be found to replace those that are being forfeited. It is still too early to say how the Panamanian government is meeting this challenge.

One controversial example that has figured prominently in the U.S. media is the granting of a long-term concession to operate the country's two key ports—Balboa on the Pacific side and Colón on the Atlantic coast—to Hutchison Port Holdings (HPH), a Hong Kong–based conglomerate. HPH is the largest port container company in the world; its other installations include Felixstowe in the United Kingdom, Freeport in the Bahamas, and Shanghai. The choice of HPH by the Panamanian government aroused criticism in the United States on two counts. The first was HPH's alleged links to the People's Republic of China, which its executives deny—notwithstanding that since the withdrawal of the British from Hong Kong the point is somewhat moot. The second is that the bidding process was less than transparent ("unorthodox" was the way the U.S. Embassy put it). As columnist Georgie Anne Geyer commented, "Panama preemptorily closed the bidding, secretly changed the rules, and simply awarded the contract to Hutchison before the American or other firms could even know what was happening."[34]

The Panamanian government points to the fact that Hutchison's bid of $22 million greatly exceeded its principal American rival, Bechtel Enterprises, which came in at $5 million. Moreover, Bechtel wanted the Panama railroad thrown in with both ports, which the Panamanian authorities felt would amount to granting an undesirable strategic monopoly. They also remind their American critics that, rightly or wrongly, the charter of the National Ports Authority does not oblige it to engage in competitive bidding.[35]

For its part, the U.S. government, though unhappy with the procedure, conceded that the HPH contract represented no prejudice to U.S. security interests. Indeed, one of its clauses specifically states that none of its provisos may be interpreted in a manner contrary to the Panamanian Constitution or the Panamanian Canal Authority organic law, both of which in different ways guarantee safe operation and maintenance of the Panama Canal.

Even if the most overheated accusations concerning Communist Chinese involvement in the ports were true, it is difficult to see how the United States could reasonably object. If the canal treaties are respected, ownership or control of specific concessions within the republic should be a matter of official indifference. Were a serious national security issue to arise, presumably U.S. concerns would be amply protected by the neutrality treaty. Fortunately for the United States, the cold war is over, and full devolution of the canal and the zone can hardly compromise its security. Had history turned out a bit differently, on occasion the United States and Panama might well have clashed over different interpretations of the neutrality treaty. As it is, one of the rights Panama presumably acquired in Carter-Torrijos was that of reaching agreements with other nations unsatisfying or even unacceptable to the United States. Fortunately for the latter, Panama's opportunities to exercise its rights in this regard are of minimal consequence to Washington.

The Hutchison Whampoa deal does, however, raise some disturbing questions about the *quality* of the privatization process in Panama. Racing pell-mell to dispose of as many properties as possible before the year 2000, the government may have become excessively careless in defining the boundaries of what it is selling. According to one report, some 100 acres of valuable real estate set aside for a railway modernization project were also granted to Hutchison Whampoa. Another study asserts that "developers of a new airport and a shopping mall may also have claims to pieces of the same parcel."[36] Barletta's tendency to exaggerate, distort, and artfully misrepresent the operations of his agency offer a valuable mine for investigative journalists, now and in the future.[37]

The Treaties in Retrospect

Whatever difficulties or inconveniences the United States may experience with Panama over the next few years, refusing to negotiate or rejecting the Carter-Torrijos treaties would hardly have served the U.S. national interest. While General Torrijos may have been bluffing when he threatened to blow up the canal if the U.S. Senate refused ratification, to call that bluff would have been expensive and dangerous. In the best of cases, the United States would have been forced to fortify the zone, militarize the canal operation, and expend enormous efforts to neutralize the political fall-out in Latin America and elsewhere.

The United States is actually rather well situated to adjust to the changes resulting from the transfer. The U.S. economy is large and innovative, and its shipping industry capable of shifting to other modes of transportation if the transisthmian route becomes too slow or too expensive. The end of the cold war and the closing of U.S. bases downgrade the geopolitical importance of Panama and demote it to the status of an ordinary (or almost ordinary) Central American country, whose portfolio can be entrusted to the care of junior foreign service officers and just-above-entry-level functionaries at the international lending organizations. Even the creation of a disingenuously styled "multilateral" drug center will not significantly cushion Panama's fall in the hierarchy of U.S. concerns, though the apparently endless quest for a totemic American "presence" raises serious questions about the country's capacity for genuinely independent life.

This leaves a very small country with some very large tasks ahead of it. Consider for a moment what Panama must accomplish within the next two years and beyond. It must replace the income from the U.S. military bases with thousands of well-paying jobs pegged to U.S. civil service rates of remuneration. (Panama's minimum wage is approximately $1 an hour.) It must dispose of millions, possibly even billions of dollars' worth of properties in an orderly and expeditious manner or expend $20 million–40 million a year in maintaining them in mothball status. Panama must reverse negative ecological trends in the Chagrés River Basin or face serious water shortages, not only in its large urban areas but in the canal itself, where growing quantities of fresh water are essential to effective navigation.

The government must maintain the canal—an old facility—in pristine condition, give adequate attention to maintenance, and insulate its management from potentially destructive patronage politics. It must balance the need for revenues with the imperative of remaining competitive with other modes of transportation. To this end, Panama must set aside large amounts of money over a multiyear period for capital improvements. Meanwhile, it must dampen the expectations that its political class has raised for generations that the canal and, lately, the reverted areas are a kind of piñata, with something for everyone.[38] The government must inspire in the foreign investment community the kind of confidence derived from the unspoken understanding that the United States—ever present in the form of a garrison 10,000 strong—would never permit the country to lapse into instability or chaos. It must address issues of economic reform, privatization, and government efficiency—even if it means laying off thousands of unproductive government employees and ending subsidized services. Above all, Panama must learn to live without the United States as a stopgap and scapegoat. These are tall orders, and one can only hope that for its own sake Panama can meet them.

"We can't make Panama succeed" after the year 2000, an American official was recently quoted as saying. "But we can't afford to let [it] fail."[39] This is precisely the opposite of the truth. The Carter-Torrijos treaties are predicated on the assumption that Panama has the right to fail—or succeed—on its own merits and as a consequence of its own actions. In that sense, the treaties represent a liberation, not just for Panama, but for the United States, which for too long assumed responsibilities in the isthmus, and indeed elsewhere in the region, for outcomes over which it always lacked adequate control.

Appendix

——————————— ✦ ———————————

Texts of Treaties Relating to the Panama Canal

Panama Canal Treaty

The United States of America and the Republic of Panama

Acting in the spirit of the Joint Declaration of April 3, 1964, by the Representatives of the Governments of the United States of America and the Republic of Panama, and of the Joint Statement of Principles of February 7, 1974, initialed by the Secretary of State of the United States of America and the Foreign Minister of the Republic of Panama, and

Acknowledging the Republic of Panama's sovereignty over its territory,

Having decided to terminate the prior Treaties pertaining to the Panama Canal and to conclude a new Treaty to serve as the basis for a new

From U.S. Department of State, *Selected Documents*, no. 6a (Washington, D.C., 1978).

relationship between them and, accordingly, have agreed upon the following:

ARTICLE I

ABROGATION OF PRIOR TREATIES AND ESTABLISHMENT OF A NEW RELATIONSHIP

1. Upon its entry into force, this Treaty terminates and supersedes:

   (a) the Isthmian Canal Convention between the United States of America and the Republic of Panama, signed at Washington, November 18, 1903;

   (b) the Treaty of Friendship and Cooperation signed at Washington, March 2, 1936, and the Treaty of Mutual Understanding and Cooperation, and the related Memorandum of Understandings Reached, signed at Panama, January 25, 1955, between the United States of America and the Republic of Panama;

   (c) All other treaties, conventions, agreements and exchanges of notes between the United States of America and the Republic of Panama concerning the Panama Canal which were in force prior to the entry into force of this Treaty; and

   (d) Provisions concerning the Panama Canal which appear in other treaties, conventions, agreements and exchanges of notes between the United States of America and the Republic of Panama which were in force prior to the entry into force of this treaty.

2. In accordance with the terms of this Treaty and related agreements, the Republic of Panama, as territorial sovereign, grants to the United States of America, for the duration of this Treaty, the rights necessary to regulate the transit of ships through the Panama Canal, and to manage, operate, maintain, improve, protect and defend the Canal. The Republic of Panama guarantees to the United States of America the

peaceful use of the land and water areas which it has been granted the rights to use for such purposes pursuant to this Treaty and related agreements.

3. The Republic of Panama shall participate increasingly in the management and protection and defense of the Canal, as provided in this Treaty.

4. In view of the special relationship established by this Treaty, the United States of America and the Republic of Panama shall cooperate to assure the uninterrupted and efficient operation of the Panama Canal.

ARTICLE II

RATIFICATION, ENTRY INTO FORCE, AND TERMINATION

1. This Treaty shall be subject of ratification in accordance with the constitutional procedures of the two Parties. The instruments of ratification of this Treaty shall be exchanged at Panama at the same time as the instruments of ratification of the Treaty Concerning the Permanent Neutrality and Operation of the Panama Canal, signed this date, are exchanged. This Treaty shall enter into force, simultaneously with the Treaty Concerning the Permanent Neutrality and Operation of the Panama Canal, six calendar months from the date of the exchange of the instruments of ratification.

2. This Treaty shall terminate at noon, Panama time, December 31, 1999.

ARTICLE III

CANAL OPERATION AND MANAGEMENT

1. The Republic of Panama, as territorial sovereign, grants to the United States of America the rights to manage, operate, and maintain the Panama Canal, its complementary works, installations and equipment and to provide for the orderly

transit of vessels through the Panama Canal. The United States of America accepts the grant of such rights and undertakes to exercise them in accordance with this Treaty and related agreements.

2. In carrying out the foregoing responsibilities, the United States of America may:

   (a) Use for the aforementioned purposes, without cost except as provided in this Treaty, the various installations and areas (including the Panama Canal) and waters, described in the Agreement in Implementation of this Article, signed this date, as well as such other areas and installations as are made available to the United States of America under this Treaty and related agreements, and take the measures necessary to ensure sanitation of such areas;

   (b) Make such improvements and alterations to the aforesaid installations and areas as it deems appropriate, consistent with the terms of this Treaty;

   (c) Make and enforce all rules pertaining to the passage of vessels through the Canal and other rules with respect to navigation and maritime matters, in accordance with this Treaty and related agreements. The Republic of Panama will lend its cooperation, when necessary, in the enforcement of such rules;

   (d) Establish, modify, collect and retain tolls for the use of the Panama Canal, and other charges, and establish and modify methods of their assessment;

   (e) Regulate relations with employees of the United States Government;

   (f) Provide supporting services to facilitate the performance of its responsibilities under this Article;

(g) Issue and enforce regulations for the effective exercise of the rights and responsibilities of the United States of America under this Treaty and related agreements. The Republic of Panama will lend its cooperation, when necessary, in the enforcement of such rules; and

(h) Exercise any other rights granted under this Treaty, or otherwise agreed upon between the two Parties.

3. Pursuant to the foregoing grant of rights, the United States of America shall, in accordance with the terms of this Treaty and the provisions of United States law, carry out its responsibilities by means of a United States Government agency called the Panama Canal Commission, which shall be constituted by and in conformity with the laws of the United States of America.

(a) The Panama Canal Commission shall be supervised by a Board composed of nine members, five of whom shall be nationals of the United States of America, and four of whom shall be Panamanian nationals proposed by the Republic of Panama for appointment to such positions by the United States of America in a timely manner.

(b) Should the Republic of Panama request the United States of America to remove a Panamanian national from membership on the Board, the United States of America shall agree to such request. In that event, the Republic of Panama shall propose another Panamanian national for appointment by the United States of America to such position in a timely manner. In case of removal of a Panamanian member of the Board at the initiative of the United States of America, both parties will consult in advance in order to reach agreement concerning such removal, and the Republic of Panama shall propose another Panamanian national for appointment by the United States of America in his stead.

(c) The United States of America shall employ a national of the United States of America as Administrator of the Panama Canal Commission, and a Panamanian national as Deputy Administrator, through December 31, 1989. Beginning January 1, 1990, a Panamanian national shall be employed as the Administrator and a national of the United States of America shall occupy the position of Deputy Administrator. Such Panamanian nationals shall be proposed to the United States of America by the Republic of Panama for appointment to such positions by the United States of America.

(d) Should the United States of America remove the Panamanian national from his position as Deputy Administrator, or Administrator, the Republic of Panama shall propose another Panamanian national for appointment to such position by the United States of America.

4. An illustrative description of the activities the Panama Canal Commission will perform in carrying out the responsibilities and rights of the United States of America under this Article is set forth in the Annex. Also set forth in the Annex are procedures for the discontinuance or transfer of those activities performed prior to the entry into force of this Treaty by the Panama Canal Company or the Canal Zone Government which are not to be carried out by the Panama Canal Commission.

5. The Panama Canal Commission shall reimburse the Republic of Panama for the costs incurred by the Republic of Panama in providing the following public services in the Canal operating areas and in housing areas set forth in the Agreement in Implementation of Article III of this Treaty and occupied by both United States and Panamanian citizen employees of the Panama Canal Commission: police, fire protection, street maintenance, street lighting, street cleaning, traffic management, and garbage collection. The Panama Canal Commission shall pay the Republic of Panama the sum of ten million United States dollars ($10,000,000) per annum for

the foregoing services. It is agreed that every three years from the date that this Treaty enters into force, the costs involved in furnishing said services shall be reexamined to determine whether adjustment of the annual payment should be made because of inflation and other relevant factors affecting the cost of such services.

6. The Republic of Panama shall be responsible for providing, in all areas comprising the former Canal Zone, services of a general jurisdictional nature such as customs and immigration, postal services, courts and licensing, in accordance with this Treaty and related agreements.

7. The United States of America and the Republic of Panama shall establish a Panama Canal Consultative Committee, composed of an equal number of high-level representatives of the United States of America and the Republic of Panama, and which may appoint such subcommittees as it may deem appropriate. This Committee shall advise the United States of America and the Republic of Panama on matters of policy affecting the Canal's operation. In view of both Parties' special interest in the continuity and efficiency of the Canal operation in the future, the Committee shall advise on matters such as general tolls policy, employment and training policies to increase the participation of Panamanian nationals in the operation of the Canal, and international policies on matters concerning the Canal. The Committee's recommendations shall be transmitted to the two Governments, which shall give such recommendations full consideration in the formulation of such policy decisions.

8. In addition to the participation of Panamanian nationals at high management levels of the Panama Canal Commission, as provided for in paragraph 3 of this Article, there shall be growing participation of Panamanian nationals at all other levels and areas of employment in the aforesaid commission, with the objective of preparing, in an orderly and efficient fashion, for the assumption by the Republic of Panama of full responsibility for the management, operation, and maintenance of the Canal upon the termination of this Treaty.

9. The use of the areas, waters and installations with respect to which the United States of America is granted rights pursuant to this Article, and the rights and legal status of United States Government agencies and employees operating in the Republic of Panama pursuant to this Article, shall be governed by the Agreement in Implementation of this Article, signed this date.

10. Upon entry into force of this Treaty, the United States Government agencies known as the Panama Canal Company and the Canal Zone Government shall cease to operate within the territory of the Republic of Panama that formerly constituted the Canal Zone.

ARTICLE IV

PROTECTION AND DEFENSE

1. The United States of America and the Republic of Panama commit themselves to protect and defend the Panama Canal. Each Party shall act, in accordance with its constitutional processes, to meet the danger resulting from an armed attack or other actions which threaten the security of the Panama Canal or of ships transiting it.

2. For the duration of this Treaty, the United States of America shall have primary responsibility to protect and defend the Canal. The rights of the United States of America to station, train, and move military forces within the Republic of Panama are described in the Agreement in Implementation of this Article, signed this date. The use of areas and installations and the legal status of the armed forces of the United States of America in the Republic of Panama shall be governed by the aforesaid Agreement.

3. In order to facilitate the participation and cooperation of the armed forces of both Parties in the protection and defense of the Canal, the United States of America and the Republic of

Panama shall establish a Combined Board comprised of an equal number of senior military representatives of each Party. These representatives shall be charged by their respective governments with consulting and cooperating on all matters pertaining to the protection and defense of the Canal, and with planning for actions to be taken in concert for that purpose. Such combined protection and defense arrangements shall not inhibit the identity or lines of authority of the armed forces of the United States of America or the Republic of Panama. The Combined Board shall provide for coordination and cooperation concerning such matters as:

(a) The preparation of contingency plans for the protection and defense of the Canal based upon the cooperative efforts of the armed forces of both parties;

(b) The planning and conduct of combined military exercises; and

(c) The conduct of United States and Panamanian military operations with respect to the protection and defense of the Canal.

4. The Combined Board shall, at five-year intervals throughout the duration of this Treaty, review the resources being made available by the two Parties for the protection and defense of the Canal. Also, the Combined Board shall make appropriate recommendations to the two Governments respecting projected requirements, the efficient utilization of available resources of the two Parties, and other matters of mutual interest with respect to the protection and defense of the Canal.

5. To the extent possible consistent with its primary responsibility for the protection and defense of the Panama Canal, the United States of America will endeavor to maintain its armed forces in the Republic of Panama in normal times at a level not in excess of that of the armed forces of the United States of America in the territory of the former Canal Zone immediately prior to the entry into force of this Treaty.

ARTICLE V

PRINCIPLE OF NON-INTERVENTION

Employees of the Panama Canal Commission, their dependents and designated contractors of the Panama Canal Commission, who are nationals of the United States of America, shall respect the laws of the Republic of Panama and abstain from any activity incompatible with the spirit of this Treaty. Accordingly, they shall abstain from any political activity in the Republic of Panama as well as any intervention in the internal affairs of the Republic of Panama. The United States of America shall take all measures within its authority to ensure that the provisions of this Article are fulfilled.

ARTICLE VI

PROTECTION OF THE ENVIRONMENT

1. The United States of America and the Republic of Panama commit themselves to implement this Treaty in a manner consistent with the protection of the natural environment of the Republic of Panama. To this end, they shall consult and cooperate with each other in all appropriate ways to ensure that they shall give due regard to the protection and conservation of the environment.

2. A Joint Commission on the Environment shall be established with equal representation from the United States of America and the Republic of Panama, which shall periodically review the implementation of this Treaty and shall recommend as appropriate to the two Governments ways to avoid or, should this not be possible, to mitigate the adverse environmental impacts which might result from their respective actions pursuant to the Treaty.

3. The United States of America and the Republic of Panama shall furnish the Joint Commission on the Environment complete information on any action taken in accordance with this Treaty which, in the judgement of both, might have significant effect on the environment. Such information shall be made available to the Commission as far in advance of the

contemplated action as possible to facilitate the study by the Commission of any potential environmental problems and to allow for consideration of the recommendation of the Commission before the contemplated action is carried out.

ARTICLE VII

FLAGS

1. The entire territory of the Republic of Panama, including the areas the use of which the Republic of Panama makes available to the United States of America pursuant to this Treaty and related agreements, shall be under the flag of the Republic of Panama, and consequently such flag always shall occupy the position of honor.

2. The flag of the United States of America may be displayed, together with the flag of the Republic of Panama, at the headquarters of the Panama Canal Commission, at the site of the Combined Board, and as provided in the Agreement in Implementation of Article IV of this Treaty.

3. The flag of the United States of America also may be displayed at other places and on some occasions, as agreed by both Parties.

ARTICLE VIII

PRIVILEGES AND IMMUNITIES

1. The installations owned or used by the agencies or instrumentalities of the United States of America operating in the Republic of Panama pursuant to this Treaty and related agreements, and their official archives and documents, shall be inviolable. The two Parties shall agree on procedures to be followed in the conduct of any criminal investigation at such locations by the Republic of Panama.

2. Agencies and instrumentalities of the Government of the United States of America operating in the Republic of Panama pursuant to this Treaty and related agreements shall be immune from jurisdiction of the Republic of Panama.

3. In addition to such other privileges and immunities as are afforded to employees of the United States Government and their dependents pursuant to this Treaty, the United States of America may designate up to twenty officials of the Panama Canal Commission who, along with their dependents, shall enjoy the privileges and immunities accorded to diplomatic agents and their dependents under international law and practice. The United States of America shall furnish to the Republic of Panama a list of the names of said officials and their dependents, identifying the positions they occupy in the Government of the United States of America, and shall keep such list current at all times.

ARTICLE IX

APPLICABLE LAWS AND LAW ENFORCEMENT

1. In accordance with the provisions of this Treaty and related agreements, the law of the Republic of Panama shall apply in the areas made available for the use of the United States of America pursuant to this Treaty. The law of the Republic of Panama shall be applied to matters or events which occurred in the former Canal Zone prior to the entry into force of this Treaty only to the extent specifically provided in prior treaties and agreements.

2. Natural or juridical persons who, on the date of entry into force of this Treaty, are engaged in business or non-profit activities at locations in the former Canal Zone may continue such business or activities at those locations under the same terms and conditions prevailing prior to the entry into force of this Treaty for a thirty-month transition period from its entry into force. The Republic of Panama shall maintain the same operating conditions as those applicable to the aforementioned enterprises prior to the entry into force of this Treaty in order that they may receive licenses to do business in the Republic of Panama subject to their compliance with the requirements of its law. Thereafter, such persons shall receive the same treatment under the law of the Republic of Panama as similar enterprises already

established in the rest of the territory of the Republic of Panama without discrimination.

3. The rights of ownership, as recognized by the United States of America, enjoyed by natural or juridical private persons in buildings and other improvements to real property located in the former Canal Zone shall be recognized by the Republic of Panama in conformity with its laws.

4. With respect to buildings and other improvements to real property located in the Canal operating areas, housing areas or other areas subject to the licensing procedure established in Article IV of the Agreement in Implementation of Article III of this Treaty, the owners shall be authorized to continue using the land upon which their property is located in accordance with the procedures established in that Article.

5. With respect to buildings and other improvements to real property located in areas of the former Canal Zone to which the aforesaid licensing procedure is not applicable, or may cease to be applicable during the lifetime or upon termination of this Treaty, the owners may continue to use the land upon which their property is located, subject to the payment of a reasonable charge to the Republic of Panama. Should the Republic of Panama decide to sell such land, the owners of the buildings or other improvements located thereon shall be offered a first option to purchase such land at a reasonable cost. In the case of non-profit enterprises, such as churches and fraternal organizations, the cost of purchase will be nominal in accordance with the prevailing practice in the rest of the territory of the Republic of Panama.

6. If any of the aforementioned persons are required by the Republic of Panama to discontinue their activities or vacate their property for public purposes, they shall be compensated at fair market value by the Republic of Panama.

7. The provisions of paragraphs 2–6 above shall apply to natural or juridical persons who have been engaged in business or

non-profit activities in locations in the former Canal Zone for at least six months prior to the date of signature of this Treaty.

8.   The Republic of Panama shall not issue, adopt or enforce any law, decree, regulation, or international agreement or take any other action which purports to regulate or would otherwise interfere with the exercise on the part of the United States of America of any right granted under this Treaty or related Agreements.

9.   Vessels transiting the Canal, and cargo, passengers and crews carried on such vessels shall be exempt from any taxes, fees, or other charges by the Republic of Panama. However, in the event such vessels call at a Panamanian port, they may be assessed charges incident thereto, such as charges for services provided to the vessel. The Republic of Panama may also require the passengers and crew disembarking from such vessels to pay such taxes, fees and charges as are established under Panamanian law for persons entering its territory. Such taxes, fees and charges shall be assessed on a nondiscriminatory basis.

10.   The United States of America and the Republic of Panama will cooperate in taking such steps as may from time to time be necessary to guarantee the security of the Panama Canal Commission, its property, its employees and their dependents, and their property, the Forces of the United States of America and the members thereof, the civilian components of the United States Forces, the dependents of members of the Forces and the civilian component, and their property, and the contractors of the Panama Canal Commission and of the United States Forces, their dependents, and their property. The Republic of Panama will seek from its Legislative Branch such legislation as may be needed to carry out the foregoing purposes and to punish any offenders.

11.   The Parties shall conclude an agreement whereby nationals of either State, who are sentenced by the courts of the other State, and who are not domiciled therein, may elect to serve their sentences in their State of nationality.

ARTICLE X

EMPLOYMENT WITHIN THE PANAMA CANAL COMMISSION

1. In exercising its rights and fulfilling its responsibilities as the employer, the United States of America shall establish employment and labor regulations which shall contain the terms, conditions and prerequisites for all categories of employees of the Panama Canal Commission. These regulations shall be provided to the Republic of Panama prior to their entry into force.

2. (a) The regulations shall establish a system of preferences when hiring employees, for Panamanian applicants possessing the skills and qualifications required for employment by the Panama Canal Commission. The United States of America shall endeavor to ensure that the number of Panamanian nationals employed by the Panama Canal Commission in relation to the total number of its employees will conform to the proportion established for foreign enterprises under the law of the Republic of Panama.

    (b) The terms and conditions of employment to be established will in general be no less favorable to persons already employed by the Panama Canal Company or Canal Zone Government prior to the entry into force of this Treaty, than those in effect immediately prior to that date.

3. (a) The United States of America shall establish an employment policy for the Panama Canal Commission that shall generally limit recruitment of personnel outside the Republic of Panama to persons possessing requisite skills and qualifications which are not available in the Republic of Panama.

    (b) The United States of America will establish training programs for Panamanian employees and apprentices in order to increase the number of Panamanian nationals qualified to assume positions within the Panama Canal Commission, as positions become available.

(c) Within five years from the entry into force of this Treaty, the number of United States nationals employed by the Panama Canal Commission who were previously employed by the Panama Canal Company shall be at least twenty percent less than the total number of United States nationals working for the Panama Canal Company immediately prior to the entry into force of this Treaty.

(d) The United States of America shall periodically inform the Republic of Panama, through the Coordinating Committee, established pursuant to the Agreement in Implementation of Article III of this Treaty, of available positions within the Panama Canal Commission. The Republic of Panama shall similarly provide the United States of America any information it may have as to the availability of Panamanian nationals claiming to have skills and qualifications that might be required by the Panama Canal Commission, in order that the United States of America may take this information into account.

4. The United States of America will establish qualification standards for skills, training and experience required by the Panama Canal Commission. In establishing such standards, to the extent they include a requirement for a professional license, the United States of America, without prejudice to its right to require additional professional skills and qualifications, shall recognize the professional licenses issued by the Republic of Panama.

5. The United States of America shall establish a policy for the periodic rotation, at a maximum of every five years, of United States citizen employees, hired after the entry into force of this Treaty. It is recognized that certain exceptions to the said policy of rotation may be made for sound administrative reasons, such as in the case of employees holding positions requiring certain non-transferable or non-recruitable skills.

6. With regard to wages and fringe benefits, there shall be no discrimination on the basis of nationality, sex or race.

Payments by the Panama Canal Commission of additional remuneration, or the provision of other benefits, such as home leave benefits, to United States nationals employed prior to entry into force of this Treaty, or to persons of any nationality, including Panamanian nationals who are thereafter recruited outside of the Republic of Panama and who change their place and residence, shall not be considered to be discrimination for purposes of this paragraph.

7. Persons employed by the Panama Canal Company or Canal Zone Government prior to the entry into force of this Treaty, who are displaced from their employment as a result of the discontinuance by the United States of America of certain activities pursuant to this Treaty, will be placed by the United States of America, to the maximum extent feasible, in other appropriate jobs with the Government of the United States, in accordance with United States Civil Service regulations. For such persons who are not United States nationals, placement efforts will be confined to United States Government activities located within the Republic of Panama. Likewise, persons previously employed in activities for which the Republic of Panama assumes responsibility as the result of this Treaty will be continued in their employment to the maximum extent feasible by the Republic of Panama. The Republic of Panama shall, to the maximum extent feasible, ensure that the terms and conditions of employment applicable to personnel employed in the activities for which it assumes responsibility are no less favorable than those in effect immediately prior to the entry into force of this Treaty. Non-United States nationals employed by the Panama Canal Company or Canal Zone Government prior to the entry into force of this Treaty who are involuntarily separated from their positions because of the discontinuance of an activity by reason of this Treaty, who are not entitled to an immediate annuity under the United States Civil Service Retirement System, and for whom continued employment in the Republic of Panama by the Government of the United States of America is not practicable, will be provided special job placement assistance by the Republic of Panama for employment in positions for which they may be qualified by experience and training.

8.   The Parties agree to establish a system whereby the Panama Canal Commission may, if deemed mutually convenient or desirable by the two Parties, assign certain employees of the Panama Canal Commission, for a limited period of time, to assist in the operation of activities transferred to the responsibility of the Republic of Panama as a result of this Treaty or related agreements. The salaries and other costs of employment of any such persons assigned to provide such assistance shall be reimbursed to the United States of America by the Republic of Panama.

9.   (a) The right of employees to negotiate collective contracts with the Panama Canal Commission is recognized. Labor relations with employees of the Panama Canal Commission shall be conducted in accordance with forms of collective bargaining established by the United States of America after consultation with employee unions.

(b) Employee unions shall have the right to affiliate with international labor organizations.

10.   The United States of America will provide an appropriate early optional retirement program for all persons employed by the Panama Canal Company or Canal Zone Government immediately prior to the entry into force of this Treaty. In this regard, taking into account the unique circumstances created by the provisions of this Treaty, including its duration, and their effect upon such employees, the United States of America shall, with respect to them:

(a) determine that conditions exist which invoke applicable United States law permitting early retirement annuities and apply such law for a substantial period of the duration of the Treaty;

(b) seek special legislation to provide more liberal entitlement to, and calculation of, retirement annuities than is currently provided for by law.

ARTICLE XI

PROVISIONS FOR THE TRANSITION PERIOD

1. The Republic of Panama shall reassume plenary jurisdiction over the former Canal Zone upon entry into force of this Treaty and in accordance with its terms. In order to provide for an orderly transition to the full application of the jurisdictional arrangements established by this Treaty and related agreements, the provisions of this Article shall become applicable upon the date this Treaty enters into force, and shall remain in effect for thirty calendar months. The authority granted to the United States of America for this transition period shall supplement, and is not intended to limit, the full application and effect of the rights and authority granted to the United States of America elsewhere in this Treaty and in related agreements.

2. During this transition period, the criminal and civil laws of the United States of America shall apply concurrently with those of the Republic of Panama in certain of the areas and installations made available for the use of the United States of America pursuant to this Treaty, in accordance with the following provisions:

   (a) The Republic of Panama permits the authorities of the United States of America to have the primary right to exercise criminal jurisdiction over United States citizen employees of the Panama Canal Commission and their dependents, and members of the United States Forces and civilian component and their dependents, in the following cases:

   (i) for any offense committed during the transition period within such areas and installations, and,

   (ii) for any offense committed prior to that period in the former Canal Zone

   The Republic of Panama shall have the primary right to

exercise jurisdiction over all other offenses committed by such persons, except as otherwise provided in this Treaty and related agreements or as may be otherwise agreed.

(b)   Either party may waive its primary right to exercise jurisdiction in a specific case or category of cases.

3.   The United States of America shall retain the right to exercise jurisdiction in criminal cases relating to offenses committed prior to the entry into force of this Treaty in violation of the laws applicable in the former Canal Zone.

4.   For the transition period, the United States of America shall retain police authority and maintain a police force in the aforementioned areas and installations. In such areas, the police authorities of the United States of America may take into custody any person not subject to their primary jurisdiction if such person is believed to have committed or to be committing an offense against applicable laws and regulations, and shall promptly transfer custody to the police authorities of the Republic of Panama. The United States of America and the Republic of Panama shall establish joint police patrols in agreed areas. Any arrests conducted by a joint patrol shall be the responsibility of the patrol member or members representing the Party having primary jurisdiction over the person or persons arrested.

5.   The courts of the United States of America and related personnel, functioning in the former Canal Zone prior to the entry into force of this Treaty, may continue to function during the transition period for the judicial enforcement of the jurisdiction to be exercised by the United States of America in accordance with this Article.

6.   In civil cases, the civilian courts of the United States of America in the Republic of Panama shall have no jurisdiction over new cases of a private civil nature, but shall retain full jurisdiction during the transition period to dispose of any civil cases, including admiralty cases, already instituted and pending before the courts prior to the entry into force of this Treaty.

7. The laws, regulations, and administrative authority of the United States of America applicable in the former Canal Zone immediately prior to the entry into force of this Treaty shall, to the extent not inconsistent with this Treaty and related agreements, continue in force for the purpose of the exercise by the United States of America of law enforcement and judicial jurisdiction only during the transition period. The United States of America may amend, repeal, or otherwise change such laws, regulations and administrative authority. The two Parties shall consult concerning procedural and substantive matters relative to the implementation of this Article, including the disposition of cases pending at the end of the transition period and, in this respect, may enter into appropriate agreements by an exchange of notes or other instrument.

8. During this transition period, the United States of America may continue to incarcerate individuals in the areas and installations made available for the use of the United States of America by the Republic of Panama pursuant to this Treaty and related agreements, or to transfer them to penal facilities in the United States of America to serve their sentences.

ARTICLE XII

A SEA-LEVEL CANAL OR A THIRD LANE OF LOCKS

1. The United States of America and the Republic of Panama recognize that a sea-level canal may be important for international navigation in the future. Consequently, during the duration of this Treaty, both Parties commit themselves to study jointly the feasibility of a sea-level canal in the Republic of Panama, and in the event they determine that such a waterway is necessary, they shall negotiate terms, agreeable to both parties, for its construction.

2. The United States of America and the Republic of Panama agree on the following:

   (a) No new interoceanic canal shall be constructed in

the territory of the Republic of Panama during the duration of this Treaty, except in accordance with the provisions of this Treaty, or as the two Parties may otherwise agree; and

(b) During the duration of this Treaty, the United States of America shall not negotiate with third States for the right to construct an interoceanic canal on any other route in the Western Hemisphere, except as the two Parties may otherwise agree.

3. The Republic of Panama grants to the United States of America the right to add a third lane of locks to the existing Panama Canal. This right may be exercised at any time during the duration of this Treaty, provided that the United States of America has delivered to the Republic of Panama copies of the plans for such construction.

4. In the event the United States of America exercises the right granted in paragraph 3 above, it may use for that purpose, in addition to the areas otherwise made available to the United States of America pursuant to this Treaty, such other areas as the two Parties may agree upon. The terms and conditions applicable to Canal operating areas made available by the Republic of Panama for the use of the United States of America pursuant to Article III of this Treaty shall apply in a similar manner to such additional areas.

5. In the construction of the aforesaid works, the United States of America shall not use nuclear excavation techniques without the previous consent of the Republic of Panama.

ARTICLE XIII

PROPERTY TRANSFER AND ECONOMIC PARTICIPATION BY THE REPUBLIC OF PANAMA

1. Upon termination of this Treaty, the Republic of Panama shall assume total responsibility for the management, operation, and maintenance of the Panama Canal, which shall be turned

over in operating condition and free of liens and debts, except as the two Parties may otherwise agree.

2. The United States of America transfers, without charge, to the Republic of Panama, all right, title and interest the United States of America may have with respect to all real property, including non-removable improvements thereon, as set forth below:

   (a) Upon entry into force of this Treaty, the Panama Railroad and such property that was located in the former Canal Zone but that is not within the land and water areas the use of which is made available to the United States of America pursuant to this Treaty. However, it is agreed that the transfer on such date shall not include buildings and other facilities, except housing, the use of which is retained by the United States of America pursuant to this Treaty and related agreements, outside such areas;

   (b) Such property located in an area or a portion thereof at such time as the use by the United States of such area or portion thereof ceases pursuant to agreement between the two Parties.

   (c) Housing units made available for occupancy by members of the Armed Forces of the Republic of Panama in accordance with paragraph 5(b) of Annex B to the Agreement in Implementation of Article IV of this Treaty at such time as such units are made available to the Republic of Panama.

   (d) Upon termination of this Treaty, all real property and non-removable improvements that were used by the United States of America for the purposes of this Treaty and related agreements and equipment related to the management, operation and maintenance of the Canal remaining in the Republic of Panama.

3. The Republic of Panama agrees to hold the United States harmless with respect to any claims which may be made by third parties relating to rights, title and interest in such property.

4. The Republic of Panama shall receive, in addition, from the Panama Canal Commission a just and equitable return on the national resources which it has dedicated to the efficient management, operation, maintenance, and protection and defense of the Panama Canal, in accordance with the following:

(a) An annual amount to be paid out of Canal operating revenues computed at a rate of thirty hundredths of a United States dollar ($0.30) per Panama Canal net ton, or its equivalency, for each vessel transiting the Canal after the entry into force of this Treaty, for which tolls are charged. The rate of thirty hundredths of a United States dollar ($0.30) per Panama Canal net ton, or its equivalency, will be adjusted to reflect changes in the United States wholesale price index for total manufactured goods during biennial periods. The first adjustment shall take place five years after entry into force of this Treaty, taking into account the changes that occurred in such price index during the preceding two years. Thereafter, successive adjustments shall take place at the end of each biennial period. If the United States of America should decide that another indexing method is preferable, such method shall be proposed to the Republic of Panama and applied if mutually agreed.

(b) A fixed annuity of ten million United States dollars ($10,000,000) to be paid out of Canal operating revenues. This amount shall constitute a fixed expense of the Panama Canal Commission.

(c) An annual amount of up to ten million United States dollars ($10,000,000) per year, to be paid out of Canal operating revenues to the extent that such revenues exceed expenditures of the Panama Canal Commission including amounts paid pursuant to this Treaty. In the event Canal operating revenues in any year do not produce a surplus sufficient to cover this payment, the unpaid balance shall be paid from operating surpluses in future years in a manner to be mutually agreed.

ARTICLE XIV

SETTLEMENT OF DISPUTES

In the event that any question should arise between the Parties concerning the interpretation of this Treaty or related agreements, they shall make every effort to resolve the matter through consultation in the appropriate committees established pursuant to this Treaty and related agreements, or, if appropriate, through diplomatic channels. In the event the Parties are unable to resolve a particular matter through such means, they may, in appropriate cases, agree to submit the matter to conciliation, mediation, arbitration, or such other procedure for the peaceful settlement of the dispute as they may mutually deem appropriate.

DONE at Washington, this 7th day of September, 1977, in duplicate, in the English and Spanish languages, both texts being equally authentic.

ANNEX

PROCEDURES FOR THE CESSATION OR TRANSFER OF ACTIVITIES CARRIED OUT BY THE PANAMA CANAL COMPANY AND THE CANAL ZONE GOVERNMENT AND ILLUSTRATIVE LIST OF THE FUNCTIONS THAT MAY BE PERFORMED BY THE PANAMA CANAL COMMISSION

1. The laws of the Republic of Panama shall regulate the exercise of private economic activities within the areas made available by the Republic of Panama for the use of the United States of America pursuant to this Treaty. Natural or juridical persons who, at least six months prior to the date of signature of this Treaty, were legally established and engaged in the exercise of economic activities in the former Canal Zone, may continue such activities in accordance with the provisions of paragraphs 2–7 of Article IX of this Treaty.

2. The Panama Canal Commission shall not perform governmental or commercial functions as stipulated in paragraph 4 of this Annex, provided, however, that this shall not be deemed to limit in any way the right of the United

States of America to perform those functions that may be necessary for the efficient management, operation and maintenance of the Canal.

3. It is understood that the Panama Canal Commission, in the exercise of the rights of the United States of America with respect to the management, operation and maintenance of the Canal, may perform functions such as are set forth below by way of illustration:

    (a) Management of the Canal enterprise.

    (b) Aids to navigation in Canal waters and in proximity thereto.

    (c) Control of vessel movement.

    (d) Operation and maintenance of the locks.

    (e) Tug service for the transit of vessels and dredging for the piers and docks of the Panama Canal Commission.

    (f) Control of the water levels in Gatun, Alajuela (Madden) and Miraflores Lakes.

    (g) Non-commercial transportation services in Canal waters.

    (h) Meteorological and hydrographic services.

    (i) Admeasurement.

    (j) Non-commercial motor transport and maintenance.

    (k) Industrial service through the use of watchmen.

    (l) Procurement and warehousing.

    (m) Telecommunications.

    (n) Protection of the environment by preventing and controlling the spillage of oil and substances harmful to human or animal life and of the ecological equilibrium in areas used in operation of the Canal and the anchorages.

    (o) Non-commercial vessel repair.

    (p) Air conditioning services in Canal installations.

    (q) Industrial sanitation and health services.

    (r) Engineering design, construction, and maintenance of the Panama Canal Commission installations.

    (s) Dredging of the Canal channel, terminal ports, and adjacent waters.

    (t) Control of the banks and stabilizing of the slopes of the Canal.

(u) Non-commercial handling of cargo on the piers and docks of the Panama Canal Commission.

(v) Maintenance of public areas of the Panama Canal Commission, such as parks and gardens.

(w) Generation of electric power.

(x) Purification and supply of water.

(y) Marine salvage in Canal waters.

(z) Such other functions as may be necessary or appropriate to carry out, in conformity with this Treaty and related agreements, the rights and responsibilities of the United States of America with respect to the management, operation and maintenance of the Panama Canal.

4. The following activities and operations carried out by the Panama Canal Company and the Canal Zone Government shall not be carried out by the Panama Canal Commission, effective upon the dates indicated herein:

(a) Upon the date of entry into force of this Treaty:

(i) Wholesale and retail sales, including those through commissaries, food stores, department stores, optical shops and pastry shops;

(ii) The production of food and drink, including milk products and bakery products;

(iii) The operation of public restaurants and cafeterias and the sale of articles through vending machines;

(iv) The operation of movie theaters, bowling alleys, pool rooms, and other recreational and amusement facilities for the use of which a charge is payable;

(v) The operation of laundry and dry cleaning plants other than those operated for official use;

(vi) The repair and service of privately owned automobiles or the sale of petroleum or lubricants thereto, including the operation of gasoline stations, repair garages and tire repair and recapping facilities, and the repair and service of other privately owned property, including appliances, electronic devices, boats, motors, and furniture;

(vii) The operation of cold storage and freezer plants other than those operated for official use;

(viii) The operation of freight houses other than those operated for official use;

(ix) The operation of commercial services to and supply of privately owned and operated vessels, including the construction of vessels, the sale of petroleum and lubricants and the provision of water, tug services not related to the Canal or other United States Government operations, and repair of such vessels, except in situations where repairs may be necessary to remove disabled vessels from the Canal;

(x) Printing services other than those for official use;

(xi) Maritime transportation for the use of the general public;

(xii) Health and medical services provided to individuals including hospitals, leprosariums, veterinary, mortuary and cemetery services;

(xiii) Educational services not for professional training, including schools and libraries;

(xiv) Postal services;

(xv) Immigration, customs and quarantine controls, except those measures necessary to insure the sanitation of the Canal;

(xvi) Commercial pier and dock services, such as the handling of cargo and passengers; and

(xvii) Any other commercial activity of a similar nature, not related to the management, operation or maintenance of the Canal.

(b) Within thirty calendar months from the date of entry into force of this Treaty, governmental services such as:

(i) Police;
(ii) Courts; and
(iii) Prison system.

5. (a) With respect to those activities or functions described in paragraph 4 above, or otherwise agreed upon by the two Parties, which are to be assumed by the Government of the Republic of Panama or by private persons subject to its authority, the two Parties shall consult prior to the discontinuance of such activities or functions by the Panama Canal Commission to develop appropriate arrangements for the orderly transfer and continued efficient operation or conduct thereof.

(b) In the event that appropriate arrangements cannot be arrived at to ensure the continued performance of a particular activity or function described in paragraph 4 above which is necessary to the efficient management, operation or maintenance of the Canal, the Panama Canal Commission may, to the extent consistent with the other provisions of this Treaty and related agreements, continue to perform such activity or function until such arrangements can be made.

Treaty Concerning the Permanent Neutrality and Operation of the Panama Canal

The United States of America and the Republic of Panama have agreed upon the following:

ARTICLE I

The Republic of Panama declares that the Canal, as an international transit waterway, shall be permanently neutral in accordance with the regime established in this Treaty. The same regime of neutrality shall apply to any other international waterway that may be built either partially or wholly in the territory of the Republic of Panama.

ARTICLE II

The Republic of Panama declares the neutrality of the Canal in order that both in time of peace and in time of war it shall remain secure and open to peaceful transit by the vessels of all nations on terms of entire equality, so that there will be no discrimination against any nation, or its citizens or subjects, concerning the conditions or charges of transit, or for any other reason, and so that the Canal, and therefore the Isthmus of Panama, shall not be the target of reprisals in any armed conflict between other nations of the world. The foregoing shall be subject to the following requirements:

(a) Payment of tolls and other charges for transit and ancillary services, provided they have been fixed in conformity with the provisions of Article III (c);

(b) Compliance with applicable rules and regulations provided such rules and regulations are applied in conformity with the provisions of Article III;

(c) The requirement that transiting vessels commit no acts of hostility while in the Canal; and

(d) Such other conditions and restrictions as are established by this Treaty.

ARTICLE III

1. For purposes of the security, efficiency and proper maintenance of the Canal the following rules shall apply:

   (a) The Canal shall be operated efficiently in accordance with conditions of transit through the Canal, and rules and regulations that shall be just, equitable and reasonable, and limited to those necessary for safe navigation and efficient, sanitary operation of the Canal;

   (b) Ancillary services necessary for transit through the Canal shall be provided;

   (c) Tolls and other charges for transit and ancillary services shall be just, reasonable, equitable and consistent with the principles of international law;

   (d) As a pre-condition of transit, vessels may be required to establish clearly the financial responsibility and guarantees for payment of reasonable and adequate indemnification, consistent with international practice and standards, for damages resulting from acts or omissions of such vessels owned or operated by a State or for which it has acknowledged responsibility, a certification by that State that it shall observe its obligations under international law to pay for damages resulting from the act or omission of such vessels when passing through the Canal shall be deemed sufficient to establish such financial responsibility;

   (e) Vessels of war and auxiliary vessels of all nations shall at all times be entitled to transit the Canal, irrespective of their internal operation, means of propulsion, origin, destination or armament, without being subjected, as a condition of transit, to inspection, search or surveillance. However, such vessels may be required to certify that they have complied with all applicable health, sanitation and quarantine regulations. In addition, such vessels shall be entitled to refuse to disclose their internal operation, origin, armament, cargo or destination. However, auxiliary vessels may be required to present written assurances, certified by an official at a high level of the government of the State requesting the exemption, that they are owned or operated by that government and in this case are being used only on government non-commercial service.

2. For purposes of this Treaty, the terms "Canal," "vessel of war," "auxiliary vessel," "internal operation," "armament" and "inspection" shall have the meanings assigned them in Annex A to this Treaty.

ARTICLE IV

The United States of America and the Republic of Panama agree to maintain the regime of neutrality established in this Treaty, which shall be maintained in order that the Canal shall remain permanently neutral, notwithstanding the termination of any other treaties entered into by the two Contracting Parties.

ARTICLE V

After the termination of the Panama Canal Treaty, only the Republic of Panama shall operate the Canal and maintain military forces, defense sites and military installations within its national territory.

ARTICLE VI

1. In recognition of the important contributions of the United States of America and of the Republic of Panama to the construction, operation, maintenance, and protection and defense of the Canal, vessels of war and auxiliary vessels of those nations shall, notwithstanding any other provisions of this Treaty, be entitled to transit the Canal irrespective of their internal operation, means of propulsion, origin, destination, armament or cargo carried. Such vessels of war and auxiliary vessels will be entitled to transit the Canal expeditiously.

2. The United States of America, so long as it has responsibility

for the operation of the Canal, may continue to provide the Republic of Colombia toll-free transit through the Canal for its troops, vessels, and materials of war. Thereafter, the Republic of Panama may provide the Republic of Panama and the Republic of Costa Rica with the right of toll-free transit.

ARTICLE VII

1. The United States and the Republic of Panama shall jointly sponsor a resolution in the Organization of American States opening to accession by all nations of the world the Protocol to this Treaty whereby all the signatories will adhere to the objectives of this Treaty, agreeing to respect the regime of neutrality set forth herein.

2. The Organization of American States shall act as the depositary for this Treaty and related instruments.

ARTICLE VIII

This Treaty shall be subject to ratification in accordance with the constitutional procedures of the two Parties. The instruments of ratification of this Treaty shall be exchanged at Panama at the same time as the instruments of ratification of the Panama Canal Treaty, signed this date, are exchanged. This Treaty shall enter into force, simultaneously with the Panama Canal Treaty, six calendar months from the date of the exchange of the instruments of ratification.

DONE at Washington this 7th day of September, 1977, in the English and Spanish languages, both texts being equally authentic.

ANNEX A

1. "Canal" includes the existing Panama Canal, the entrances thereto and the territorial areas of the Republic of Panama adjacent thereto, as defined on the map annexed hereto and any other interoceanic waterway in which the United States of America is a participant or in which the United States of America has participated in connection with the construction

or financing, that may be operated wholly or partially within the territory of the Republic of Panama, the entrances thereto and the territorial seas adjacent thereto.

2. "Vessel of war" means a ship belonging to the naval forces of a State, and bearing the external marks distinguishing warships of its nationality, under the command of an officer duly commissioned by the government and whose name appears in the Navy List, and manned by a crew which is under regular naval discipline.

3. "Auxiliary vessel" means any ship, not a vessel of war, that is owned or operated by a State and used, for the time being, exclusively on government non-commercial service.

4. "Internal operation" encompasses all machinery and propulsion systems, as well as the management and control of the vessel, including its crew. It does not include the measures necessary to transit vessels under the control of pilots while such vessels are in the Canal.

5. "Armament" means arms, ammunitions, implements of war and other equipment of a vessel which possesses characteristics appropriate for use for warlike purposes.

6. "Inspection" includes on-board examination of vessel structure, cargo, armament, and internal operation. It does not include those measures strictly necessary for admeasurement, nor those measures strictly necessary to assure safe, sanitary transit and navigation, including examination of deck and visual navigation equipment, nor in the case of live cargoes, such as cattle or other livestock, that may carry communicable diseases, those measures necessary to assure that health and sanitation requirements are satisfied.

Notes

CHAPTER 2: THE TREATIES

1. The full text of both treaties appears in appendix A.

2. George D. Moffett III, *The Limits of Victory: The Ratification of the Panama Canal Treaties* (Ithaca, N.Y.: Cornell University Press, 1985), p. 23.

3. Here I am summarizing the excellent analysis of Moffett. A serious treatment of the canal's centrality to the security of the United States is Paul B. Ryan, *The Panama Canal Controversy: U.S. Diplomacy and Defense Interests* (Stanford: Hoover Institution Press, 1977).

4. This subject is explored at some length in chapter 2.

5. Moffett, *Limits of Victory*, p. 54

6. Ibid., p. 68

7. Ibid., p. 74

8. "Panama—Torrijos Addresses Nation Prior to Treaty Plebiscite," complete text in U.S. Senate, Committee on Foreign Relations, *Panama Canal Treaties. Part 5: Markup*, 95th Cong., 1st sess., 1978, pp. 41–42, 45.

9. *Power and Principle: Memoirs of the National Security Adviser, 1977–1981* (New York: Farrar Straus Giroux, 1983), p. 54.

10. Jeane J. Kirkpatrick, "U.S. Security in Latin America," *Commentary*, January 1981.

11. U.S. Senate Committee on Foreign Relations, *Panama Canal Treaties. Part 1: Administration Witnesses*, 95th Cong., 1st sess., 1978, pp. 326–27

12. Whereas Article 5 of the Neutrality Treaty provided that after the termination of the Panama Canal Treaty in the year 2000 "only the Republic of Panama shall ... maintain military forces, defense sites, and military installations within

its national territory," the DeConcini reservation reads that "notwithstanding the provisions of Article V ... if the Canal is closed, or its operations are interfered with, the United States of America and the Republic of Panama shall each independently have the right to take such steps as it deems necessary in accordance with its constitutional processes, including the use of military force in Panama, to reopen the Canal or restore the operations of the Canal, as the case may be."

13. A flavor of this rhetoric is afforded by the text of several speeches by Torrijos's ministers, reproduced in U.S. Senate, Committee on Foreign Relations, *Panama Canal Treaties. Part 2: Congressional Witnesses*, 95th Cong., 1st sess., 1978, pp. 14–35.

14. *Power and Principle*, p. 51.

15. See chapter 3.

16. U.S. Senate, Committee on Foreign Relations, *Panama Canal Treaties. Part 3: Public Witnesses*, 95th Cong., 1st sess., 1978, pp. 88–96.

17. An American on official business in Ecuador in the summer of 1979, meeting with a group of businessmen and politicians in the port city of Guayaquil, was pointedly asked what the United States would do about a proposed Panamanian increase in tolls, which, it was explained, would cut into the profitability of banana shipments to Western Europe. When the visitor inquired if Ecuador was one of the countries that, though publicly in favor of the Carter-Torrijos treaties, was actually opposed, the Ecuadorians hesitated and then all felt pressed to deny the possibility.

18. Senate, *Panama Canal Treaties. Part 1*, pp. 107–27. The article in question originally appeared in the *AEI Defense Review*.

19. President Ernesto Pérez Balladares chose not to journey to San José, Costa Rica, to meet President Bill Clinton along with the other Central American presidents in May 1997 precisely to underscore this point and to reassert the demand for special treatment from the United States.

CHAPTER 3: THE COUNTRY

1. The statistics quoted in this chapter come either from Inter-American Development Bank, *Economic and Social Progress in Latin America* (Washington, D.C.: 1996), United Nations Economic Commission for Latin America, *Social Panorama of Latin America* (Santiago, Chile: 1996), or Sarah W. Meditz and Dennis M. Hauratty, eds., *Panama: A Country Study* (Washington, D.C.: Library of Congress, 1989).

2. Jan Knippers Black and Edmundo Flores, "The Historical Setting," in *Panama: A Country Study*, p. 4.

3. An American army officer recently remarked on the myths and mystiques that still surround the zone, even though it was formally abolished in 1979. "The

folks up in the hills still think the streets here are paved with gold, and it always surprises them when they come into the zone for the first time and find a lot of old buildings with roofs that leak." *New York Times*, July 13, 1997.

4. The clash of cultures disguised the fact that the U.S. Supreme Court (Wilson v. Shaw, 1906, and Luckenbach v. U.S., 1926) had held that the canal was not U.S. territory and that the United States had to treat the ports of Balboa and Colón as foreign ports. U.S. citizen employees of the Canal Zone (though not military) were treated as employees in a foreign country and paid taxes on that basis. Thus, the colonial metaphor was never as perfect as politics made it seem.

5. The balboa circulates only in coins. General Noriega did contemplate printing a national currency in the late 1980s, but only under the pressing necessity to circumvent the U.S. embargo. In the event, nothing of the sort was done. His successor, Guillermo Endara, went so far as to have a local currency printed up, though it never circulated. But this was largely an essay in counteracting the charge that he was not sufficiently independent of the United States, which after all had installed him in office, rather than a response to popular demand for an independent Panamanian currency.

6. According to the U.S. Agency for International Development. Contrary to what might be supposed by critics, a relatively minor part of this total is represented by military assistance—somewhat less than 5 percent.

7. The president of the Panamanian Association of Hotels has already said publicly that the reduction of a significant number of American troops will mean an 80 percent drop in hotel employment. *El Universal de Panamá* (Panama City), May 5, 1996.

8. After the 1989 invasion, the twentieth of each month was reserved for anti-American demonstrations to protest the violation of Panamanian sovereignty and the loss of Panamanian lives and property. These continue, though somewhat attenuated since the election of President Enrique Pérez Balladares, who belongs to Torrijos's (and Noriega's) Democratic Revolutionary Party.

9. Interview on TVN, Panama City, *Foreign Broadcast Information Service—Latin America*, July 17, 1996.

10. Rob Schroth & Associates, *A Conversation with the Panamanian People* (Washington, D.C.: Rob Schroth & Associates, 1993).

11. U.S. Information Agency, "Panamanians Remain Strongly Pro-American: Want Benefits for Keeping Bases beyond 1999." Press release. Washington, D.C., March 4, 1996.

12. *La Prensa* (Panama City), December 11, 1995. If the United States were unwilling to compensate the Panamanian state for its presence, in this survey 49.8 percent would still favor the bases, with 40.2 percent opposing.

13. *La Prensa*, May 16, 1995.

14. "Some Mixed Signals for Uncle Sam," *U.S. News and World Report*, October 25, 1993.

15. U.S. Secretary of State Cyrus Vance admitted that "the Panamanian gov-

ernment has in the past been charged with abusing the civil and political rights of its citizens.... And we have discussed this issue with that Government.... Already there are encouraging signs." For Secretary Vance these "encouraging" signs were not, however, actual improvement in human rights performance, but rather invitations to the Inter-American Human Rights Commission to visit the country and to the United Nations to send observers to the upcoming plebiscite on the canal treaties! Even more disingenuous was the testimony of U.S. Ambassador William Jorden. When asked by one senator whether human rights in Panama were "worse, the same, or better under the present Torrijos government than they were before," the best he could manage is that "I have been in Panama for the last three and a half years. I was not present in Panama in the 1960s or earlier. I cannot say with assurance or from personal knowledge.... Not knowing what the situation was in that area in the 1960s or 1950s, I really would prefer to reserve an answer." U.S. Senate, *Panama Canal Treaties. Part 1: Administration Witnesses*, 95th Cong., 1st sess., 1978, pp. 14, 295.

16. The Organization of American States was more pliable, accepting the credentials of Solís Palma's ambassador to that body, thus creating a rather anomalous situation. In the process, it underscored that organization's incapacity to mediate the crisis and thus pushed the United States toward the kind of unilateral solution to which it was preternaturally disposed.

17. The most dramatic image to appear on international television after the elections was Vice-President–Elect Guillermo Ford, his shirt dripping in blood. In fact, Ford was unharmed. His bodyguard standing by had been shot by someone who had a personal score to settle with him; part of the poor man splattered onto Ford, whose gruesome image underscored—however inaccurately in this case—the brutality of the Noriega regime and shocked worldwide opinion.

18. During 1986, while working for the Kissinger Commission on Central America, I had occasion to see the National Intelligence Estimates (NIEs) on Panama, which underscored this point with droll emphasis.

19. There is a vast literature on this subject, mostly written by American journalists determined to blame the United States for Panama's misfortunes. Some examples are John Dinges, *Our Man in Panama* (New York: Random House, 1990); Frederick Kempe, *Romancing the Dictator* (New York: G. P. Putnam's, 1990), and, with a slightly less critical cutting edge, R. M. Koster and Guillermo Sánchez, *In the Time of the Tyrants: Panama: 1968–1990* (New York: W. W. Norton, 1990).

20. This effectively doubled the number of American troops in Panama, since another 12,000 were already on permanent deployment in bases there.

21. Contrary to the claims of U.S. critics of the invasion—former attorney general Ramsey Clark, Jesse Jackson, and others—there were no bombing attacks on civilian areas of Panama City. In fact, during Operation Just Cause only two bombs were dropped—from the F-117s on the Rio Hato Base. Both missed their targets.

22. When Mrs. Endara won the lottery in Panama—under circumstances so

providential as to invite universal disbelief—she was asked what she planned to do with the money. Instead of at least pretending that she would turn the proceeds over to charity, she artlessly confessed to the press that she planned to have a "wonderful Christmas." See Mark Falcoff and Richard Millett, *Searching for Panama* (Washington, D.C.: Center for Strategic and International Studies, 1993), p. 12.

23. Ibid., p. 33.

24. Carlés argued that since the neutrality treaty gave the United States the right to "enter Panama whenever they felt like it" anyway, they might as well try to coax some additional advantages out of the situation. José Salvador Muñoz, the candidate of the Authentic Panameñistas, disagreed, arguing that the presence of U.S. forces in Panama was "the cause of conflict and permanent disturbance" in the bilateral relationship and that "5,000 workers [in the Canal Zone] cannot decide on the economic future of the country." Blades said that he was personally opposed to the bases remaining but would accept a referendum on the subject if the Panamanians themselves demanded it. Pérez Balladares voiced similar views. See Mark Falcoff, *The 1994 Panamanian Elections: Pre-Election Report* (Washington, D.C.: Center for Strategic and International Studies, 1994), p. 11.

25. As Ambassador Dean Hinton put it with characteristic acerbity, "any time anything goes wrong, somebody picks up the phone and calls us to fix it." *Washington Post*, October 8, 1990.

Chapter 4: The Canal

1. U.S. Senate, Committee on Foreign Relations, *Panama Canal: Hearings. Part 4: Congressional and Public Witnesses*, 95th Cong., 1st sess., 1978, p. 123. The full report is Ely M. Brandes and Betty R. Samuel, *Panama Canal Toll Rates: Estimates of Maximum Revenues* (Palo Alto: International Research Associates, 1975). See also W. M. Whitman, *Environmental Assessment of Proposal to Increase Tolls* (Panama City: Panama Canal Company, 1976).

2. U.S. Senate, *Panama Canal: Hearings. Part 4*, p. 124.

3. Ibid., p. 128.

4. Ibid., p. 135. Senator Clifford Case remarked that, on a visit to Panama, he had been told by the head of the Panamanian planning operation that "they are expecting to be able to cut very drastically personnel costs from those that now obtain.... They said quite frankly to us ... that for various reasons they think people in the Zone are getting too much money in relation to ordinary Panamanian working people, and that they expect to equalize this to the advantage of the net return on the canal.... This is a factor in the $60 million which they hope to get out of this thing as net revenue." Ibid., p. 142.

5. Ibid., p. 141.

6. Lee Hockstader, "Officials and Shippers Question Panama's Preparation for Canal Takeover," *Washington Post*, October 17, 1990. Five years later Profes-

sor Richard Millett, perhaps the most eminent academic specialist on the region, was telling a congressional committee that the canal "cannot keep going just on shipping revenues. They are already close to the maximum tolls they can charge without becoming non-competitive with other routes.... Right now it is cheaper for U.S. ships to bunker by going all the way to Long Beach [California] than it is to fill up in Panama because of the various odd regulations involving oil, the obsolescence of the refinery." U.S. House of Representatives, Committee on International Relations, Subcommittee on the Western Hemisphere, *U.S. Strategic Interests in Panama,* Hearings, 104th Cong., 1st sess., 1995, p. 27.

7. Reuters Financial Service dispatch, August 9, 1996; *Business Times* (Singapore), September 27, 1996.

8. *Miami Herald,* September 9, 1997. "The danger is that pressure to do something about the poor in Panama becomes such a powerful element that candidates for president start making a lot of promises," declared Juan Kelly, president of the London-based International Chamber of Shipping. Panamanian politicians might well turn the canal "into a political football with their claims the country is not making enough money from it." *Journal of Commerce,* September 10, 1997.

9. "The Future of the Panama Canal," *Journal of Inter-American Studies and World Affairs,* vol. 35, no. 3 (fall 1993), pp. 121–22.

10. Hockstader, "Officials and Shippers Question Panama's Preparation."

11. President Pérez Balladares's supporters are actively trying to change the Panamanian Constitution to permit consecutive five-year terms. Under present rules, two terms must expire before a former president can again run for the highest office. Talk of this sort—which the president's disclaimers do nothing to discourage—tends to poison the government's relations with the opposition parties and to raise questions about its commitment to a nonpolitical administration of all public facilities, not just the canal.

12. For full text of the new organic law, see *La Prensa* (Panama City), May 28, 1996.

13. *New York Times,* July 13, 1997.

14. Ibid., September 28, 1997. The American deputy administrator of the canal, Joe Reeder, has rushed to Pérez Balladares's defense and has alleged that while "being a friend of the President cannot be the only credential" to membership in the canal authority, "neither should it be an impediment." Mr. Reeder missed the point entirely, intentionally or not. Precisely because the canal is so central a resource to Panama, the president should have gone out of his way to avoid even the appearance of nepotism or political favoritism. For Ritter's shady past, see *Miami Herald,* September 7, 1997.

15. James Kitfield, "Yankee, Don't Go!" *National Journal,* February 24, 1996. As Panamanian editorial writer Tomás Cabral put it with admirable candor, "If we have been unable to handle the railroad properly, what makes us think we can handle the canal?" He adds that preventive maintenance "requires working cus-

toms and methods still not incorporated into our way of living. Just look at the fleets of vehicles of the various ministries or the Public Works Ministry's heavy equipment to realize what could happen to the canal if we fail to organize ourselves immediately.... Nepotism, influence peddling, and corruption in the administration are capable of turning the Panama Canal into a heap of scrap iron in a short time." *El Panamá-América* (Panama City), February 24, 1992.

16. Hockstader, "Officials and Shippers Question Panama's Preparation." The Pérez Balladares administration has solved the problem by leasing the ports to a Chinese-based company (see chapter 5).

17. Clifford Kraus, "Panama Canal a Worry to Shippers," *New York Times*, January 22, 1991. The canal administrator, Gilberto Guardia, responded to this report in a letter to the editor on February 7, 1991. He characterized the report as "extremely misleading," focusing on "isolated negative statements by a few individuals." He took the reporter to task for not speaking to any canal company employees, insisted that the company spent $100 million annually on maintenance and improvements, and assured readers that his continuing discussions with all major users "clearly indicate their satisfaction with Canal transit services." Nonetheless, five years later, his Panamanian predecessor was admitting to the press that a "prejudice" existed among main canal users "over Panama's scarce efficiency to effectively manage the waterway." On repeated occasions, he avowed, many canal users have clearly voiced their doubts in this regard. *La Prensa* (Panama City), August 18, 1996. Just why this "prejudice" persisted he did not say.

18. Testimony of Deputy Assistant Secretary of State Anne Patterson in U.S. House of Representatives, *U.S. Strategic Interests in Panama: Hearings*, pp. 17–18.

19. Panama Canal Commission, *Master Plan to Implement the U.S. Army Corps of Engineers (USACE) Recommendations* (Panama City, 1997), pp. 2–3, 5–6.

20. *Time*, December 15, 1997.

21. As long ago as 1990, Manfredo was warning Panamanian politicians that they would have to be "prepared to recognize that a series of administrative practices employed by local public enterprises must be changed to guarantee that the Canal operates efficiently ... if politicians fail to realize the Canal does not represent an opportunity to benefit their friends with contracts, then we are on the wrong course." *La Prensa*, June 28, 1990. More recently, his successor Gilberto Guardia admitted that "there are a number of very tough decisions that still have to be made in terms of guaranteeing the financial independence of the canal agency, and its continued reliance on a merit system for its employees.... And some of those decisions will be politically difficult." Kitfield, "Yankee, Don't Go!"

22. Tripartite Commission for Studies on Alternatives to the Panama Canal, *Final Report of the Commission for the Study of Alternatives to the Panama Canal* (Washington/Panama City/Tokyo, 1993), passim. See also *El Universal*

de Panamá (Panama City), May 21, 1996.

23. Widening the cut would cost one-third less than other schemes.

24. This report was never published by the Government Printing Office. These figures are taken from the unpublished manuscript.

25. See interview with canal administrator Alberto Alemán Zubieta on Telemetro TV (Panama City), August 14, 1996. The commission recently reported that its capital program for the fiscal years 1996–1998 totaled $248 million, with an additional $228 million for FY 1999–2000. It includes six major efforts— "acceleration of the Gaillard Cut–widening project, augmentation of the tugboat fleet, design and procurement of additional locomotives, modernization of the vessel traffic management system, hydraulic conversion of the miter gates and rising stem valves moving machinery, and automation of locks machinery controls." Panama Canal Commission, *Proposal to Increase Tolls and Apply Certain Rules for the Measurement of Vessels* (Internet, 1996).

26. On the Nicaraguan route and the decisions that led to the choice of Panama, see Dana Gardner Munro, *Intervention and Dollar Diplomacy in the Caribbean, 1901–1921* (Princeton: Princeton University Press, 1964), pp. 38–42 and passim. The more recent Costa Rican project was reported in the *Financial Times* (London), July 21, 1992.

27. U.S. Senate, *Panama Canal Treaties: Hearings. Part 1,* pp. 336–51; Scott's statement, p. 373.

28. Ibid., pp. 266–67.

29. "Panama's Environment Ministry, known by its Spanish acronym— INRENARE—is regarded by many as a bad joke. Many appointments come as a reward for political support for the ruling [Democratic Revolutionary] party, leading to widespread inefficiency. Dissenters are usually fired, according to the Panama City–based Environmental Defense group and Western diplomatic sources." Jon Mitchell, "Water Woes: Deforestation Could Dry Up the Panama Canal," *Christian Science Monitor,* October 23, 1997.

30. Stanley Heckadon-Moreno, "Impact of Development on the Panama Canal Environment," *Journal of Inter-American Studies,* vol. 35, no. 3 (fall 1993), pp. 129–49. I have relied heavily on this analysis for much material in this section. See also Eric A. Greenquist, "Panama at a New Watershed," *Américas,* July 1996, and, for a somewhat more optimistic prognosis, Tensie Whelan, "The Panama Canal: Will the Watershed Hold?" *Environment,* April 1988.

31. Transcript of Jorge Ritter news conference, Panama City, Sistema de Televisión Educativa, *Foreign Broadcast Information Service–Latin America,* September 9, 1997. Efforts by canal administrator Alberto Alemán to address these questions more directly are only marginally more reassuring. Specifically, Alemán pledges to make environmental considerations the first priority of the canal authority after 1999 and to use satellite imaging to monitor the rainforest. He has also announced a $3 million fund to combat environmental problems, though it is unclear whether he means on an annual or one-time basis. (In either case, it

would fall far short of what is needed.) "Even under the best political conditions," one American journalist reports, "the upper and lower watersheds are an administrative nightmare, encompassing two provinces, eight districts, and 33 local councils. This is aside from falling under the [competing] jurisdiction of the Environment Ministry, the Interoceanic Regional Authority (ARI), and the PCC itself." He quotes a research biologist with one environmental organization in Panama City as saying that "if politics [as they are now] are involved in the management of the canal, it will be disastrous." Mitchell, "Water Woes."

32. *Wall Street Journal,* November 6, 1997.

33. Max Manwaring, "The Security of Panama and the Canal: Now and in the Future," *Journal of Inter-American Studies,* vol. 35, no. 3 (fall 1993), p. 154.

34. For further discussion, see chapter 5.

35. Manwaring, "Security of Panama and the Canal," p. 156.

36. For further discussion, see chapter 5.

37. This point was forcefully made by one of the principal critics of the treaties at the time of the hearings. See Roger Fontaine, "Scare Talk and the Canal," *Wall Street Journal,* August 22, 1977.

38. *La Prensa,* June 28, 1990.

39. Ibid., November 19, 1991.

40. Ibid., August 31, 1991. He reminded his fellow Panamanians that the United States until 1987 "helped to consolidate and uphold the dictatorship in Panama; therefore we had better learn to depend on ourselves."

41. *El Panamá-América,* October 31, 1990.

42. See *La Prensa,* March 25, 1991. The issue of American base retention is discussed at length in chapter 5.

43. Radio interview reproduced in *Foreign Broadcast Information Service– Latin America,* March 21, 1990.

44. *New York Times,* February 17, 1992. The study group was convened by Undersecretary of Defense Paul Wolfowitz. Its members were drawn from the Joint Chiefs of Staff, the Defense Intelligence Agency, and the policy and analytical offices of the Secretary of Defense. The Panama scenario was the only one situated in Latin America.

45. Panama was certified "in the overriding national interest," which was a way of saying that it was guilty but not sentenced.

46. U.S. Senate, Committee on Foreign Relations, Subcommittee on Terrorism, Narcotics and International Operations, *Recent Developments in Transnational Crime Affecting U.S. Law Enforcement and Foreign Policy; Mutual Legal Assistance Treaty in Criminal Matters with Panama, Treaty Doc. 102-14; and 1994 International Narcotics Control Strategy Report,* 103rd Cong., 2d sess., 1994, p. 3.

47. *La Prensa,* September 11, 1991. More recently, Gabriel Castro, national security advisor and head of the Civilian Intelligence Service, testified that some $600 million was entering Panama annually without any kind of control, presum-

ably a large part of it from drug trafficking. He estimated that $2 million a day was coming in from Colombia alone. *El Panamá-América*, November 17, 1995.

48. *La Prensa*, April 6, 1997.

49. *El Panamá-América*, June 30, 1997.

50. Ibid., July 17, 1997.

51. *La Prensa*, July 27, 1997.

52. U.S. House of Representatives, Committee on Foreign Affairs, Subcommittees on International Security, International Organizations, and Human Rights, *International Terrorism: Buenos Aires, Panama and London (Hearings)*, 103rd Cong., 2d sess., 1994, p. 29.

53. U.S. Senate, *U.S. Strategic Interests in Panama*, p. 15.

54. Ibid., pp. 16–17.

55. Testimony of General Frederick C. Smith, in U.S. Senate, *U.S. Strategic Interests in Panama*, p. 16.

56. *El Siglo* (Panama City), August 7, 1994.

57. *Estrella de Panamá* (Panama City), February 9, 1992.

58. *La Prensa*, March 23, 1991.

CHAPTER 5: THE REVISIONIST TEMPTATION

1. During the 1997 calendar year, the U.S. government planned to transfer Quarry Heights, Albrook Air Force Base, Arraijan Tank Farm, Balboa Elementary School, Gorgas Hospital, and Currundu Flats to Panama.

2. "Nothing in the treaty shall preclude the Republic of Panama and the US from making, in accordance with their respective constitutional processes, any agreement or arrangement between the two countries to facilitate performance at any time after December 31, 1999, of their responsibilities to maintain the regime of neutrality established in the Treaty, including agreements or arrangements for the stationing of any US military forces or the maintenance of defense sites after the date in Panama that Panama and the US may deem necessary or appropriate." U.S. Department of State, *Documents Associated with the Panama Canal Treaties* (Washington, D.C., 1977), p. 16.

3. They are H.R. 4 (Crane), introduced January 4, 1995; S.R. 14 (Helms), introduced September 9, 1996; H.R. 7 (Pickett), introduced January 9, 1997; H.R. 1148 (Bateman), March 20, 1997; and H.R. 1344 (Bateman), introduced April 16, 1997.

4. Atlantic Council of the United States, *Defining a New Relationship: The Issue of U.S. Access to Facilities in Panama: Policy Paper* (Washington, D.C.: ACUS, 1996), p. 23.

5. Quoted in James Kitfield, "Yankee, Don't Go!" *National Journal*, February 24, 1996. This statement was made before SouthCom headquarters were removed from Panama to Miami.

6. Gina Marie Lichacz (Hatheway), "The Future of U.S. Military Presence in Panama" (John F. Kennedy School of Government, Harvard University, 1994); Murl D. Munger, Philip A. Brehm, William W. Mendel, and J. Mark Ruhl, *U.S. Army South after Withdrawal from Panama* (Carlisle Barracks, Pa.: Strategic Studies Institute, U.S. Army War College, 1991); Lt. Gen. Victor H. Krulak, USMC, retired, ed., *Panama: An Assessment* (Washington, D.C.: U.S. Strategic Institute, 1990); U.S. House of Representatives, Committee on International Relations, Subcommittee on the Western Hemisphere, *U.S. Strategic Interests in Panama (Hearings)*, 104th Cong., 1st sess., 1995; U.S. Senate, Committee on Foreign Relations, *The Future of U.S. Military Presence in Panama*, staff report, 105th Cong., 1st sess., 1997. This report was drafted by Gina Marie Lichacz (Hatheway). To avoid confusion with her Kennedy School paper, this document is referred to as *U.S. Military Presence*.

7. Mengel et al., *U.S. Army South*, p. 33.

8. Testimony of Col. John A. Cope, U.S. Army, retired, in U.S. House, *U.S. Strategic Interests in Panama*, pp. 58–59.

9. Lichacz (Hatheway), *Future of U.S. Military Presence*, p. 20.

10. Cope in U.S. House, *U.S. Strategic Interests in Panama*, pp. 28–29.

11. Lichacz (Hatheway), *Future of U.S. Military Presence*, p. 22. The deputy director of J-5 (strategy and plans) at SouthCom confided to Mrs. Hatheway that under such circumstances the impact on U.S. military personnel would be "difficult." He suggested the following scenario: "Consider sitting down in an AWACS and going on a mission without getting off the plane. The impact of doing everything, day after day ... would come from the same squadron." The personnel assigned to the squadron who perform on a daily basis might end up on duty every third day. This would presumably have a negative effect on morale. The officer concluded that "you would have to increase the size of the military group because more of the things we do here would have to be done in host nations." Ibid., pp. 22–23.

12. U.S. Senate, *U.S. Military Presence*, pp. 6–7.

13. Ibid., p. 7. This facility has subsequently been sold by the Panamanian government to British Cable & Wireless, which presumably addresses the major technological concerns, though not necessarily the security considerations.

14. Lichacz (Hatheway), *Future of U.S. Military Presence*, pp. 23–24. To run a mission to the Beni region of Bolivia from Miami adds an additional five hours of flying time. As one officer explained, "If a U.S. military aircraft is flying a twelve to fifteen hour mission already, five additional hours will not be easy, particularly if done on a daily basis." Ibid., p. 21.

15. U.S. Senate, *U.S. Military Presence*, p. 22. Mireya Moscoso, widow of Arnulfo Arias and presidential candidate of the Arnulfista Party in 1994, was reportedly surprised during a recent visit to Chirique, about six hours' driving time from Panama City, where "many of the 'campesino' women told her that they do not want the US military to leave Panama. They mentioned to her the many projects that the US military had built for them, including schools and roads. These

projects that go unnoticed in Panama City have been beneficial to developing rural areas that have been ignored by the Panamanian government." Ibid., p. 13.

16. As Endara's Foreign Minister Julio Linares famously put it, rather than sign a treaty granting residual base rights to the United States, he would prefer to "resign and go home." *El Panamá-América* (Panama City), August 29, 1990.

17. *La Prensa* (Panama City), October 31, 1996.

18. Ibid., October 1, 1995.

19. Ibid., August 31, 1991.

20. *La Estrella de Panamá* (Panama City), September 9, 1991.

21. *La Prensa*, March 15, 1995.

22. See note 15.

23. *La Prensa*, September 16, 1991.

24. Ibid., October 3, 1995.

25. *El Siglo* (Panama City), November 13, 1996.

26. *El Panamá-América*, October 17, 1996.

27. *La Prensa*, September 26, 1991.

28. *El Universal de Panamá* (Panama City), March 30, 1996.

29. Interview with Telemetro TV, *Foreign Broadcast Information Service— Latin America*, December 4, 1995.

30. Interview with TVN, ibid., July 17, 1996.

31. *El Panamá-América*, August 1, 1991.

32. As the late foreign minister Gabriel Lewis pointed out, maintaining the reverted areas costs Panama around $40 million a year. Would it serve Panama's interest in the transition, he asked, "to do without the $200 million we get for 4,000 [American] soldiers?" *El Siglo*, October 11, 1996.

33. The MOLIRENA Party has not, however, as yet taken an official position on the subject.

34. *El Diario Independiente* (Panama City), February 14, 1991.

35. *El Panamá-América*, February 10, 1991.

36. RPC-TV, *Foreign Broadcast Information Service–Latin America*, February 14, 1992.

37. *El Panamá-América*, September 20, 1996. Vallarino has also raised the question of whether Panama—which in his view has been unable to manage adequately the assets that have reverted since 1979—is ready to take on properties three times the size of those already received and in only three years. *La Estrella de Panamá*, September 9, 1996.

38. See note 27.

39. *La Estrella de Panamá*, September 8, 1996.

40. PRC-TV, *Foreign Broadcast Information Service—Latin America*, September 17, 1996.

41. *El Siglo*, October 11, 1996.

42. The case of the Philippines seems to have been of particular interest to Panamanian advocates of U.S. basing. Alvaro Cabal Miranda calculates that if

Panama received the same annual payment as the Philippines ($1 billion), it would be able to "repay its foreign debt, finance the social security fund, build the Panama-Paso Canoa highway, repay the thirteenth month bonus [for public employees], and still have money remaining." *El Panamá-América*, August 8, 1991.

43. *El Panamá-América*, August 1, 1991.

44. *El Siglo*, December 17, 1991.

45. U.S. Senate, *U.S. Military Presence*, p. 14.

46. *El Panamá-América*, March 29, 1996.

47. Radio Soberana Civilista, *Foreign Broadcast Information Service—Latin America*, January 26, 1994.

48. XEW-TV (Mexico City), ibid., May 12, 1994.

49. As President Pérez Balladares said, "We are not going to come out and say, 'Boys, we want you to stay." *La Prensa*, April 27, 1996.

50. U.S. Senate, *U.S. Military Presence*, p. 10. See also *La Prensa*, September 25, 1996.

51. *El Panamá-América*, November 17, 1995.

52. Though critical of the Clinton administration's handling of the negotiations, the Senate report cited above is most emphatic: "Panama should not receive a direct 'quid pro quo' for negotiations as suggested by rent.... The United States should make it clear to Panama that [the] benefits which they currently take for granted will not be there beyond the year 2000 if the U.S. military cannot stay in Panama." U.S. Senate, *U.S. Military Presence*, p. 22.

53. This much was admitted by Foreign Minister Ricardo Arias in a braodcast interview on TVN, *Foreign Broadcast Information Service–Latin America*, July 17, 1996.

54. *La Estrella de Panamá*, January 10, 1997.

55. U.S. Senate; *U.S. Military Presence*, p. 13.

56. Ibid., pp. 12–13.

57. Ibid., p. 22.

58. Dissenting comments of Rogelio Novey, alternate executive director for Venezuela and Panama, Inter-American Development Bank, *Defining a New Relationship*, p. 29.

59. U.S. Senate, *U.S. Military Presence*, pp. 20–21.

60. *New York Times*, December 25, 1997.

61. Ibid.; January 7, 1998, background briefing from the Pentagon; extensive interview with President Pérez Balladares on Telemetro TV Network (Panama City), *Foreign Broadcast Information Service–Latin America*, January 1, 1998.

62. Brazil prides itself on an independent foreign policy—independent, that is, of the United States—and would be unconvinced by the "multilateral" mask. Chile's military is still smarting from a fifteen-year arms embargo slapped on it by the United States during the Pinochet dictatorship. Colombia regards Panama as *terra irredenta* and, in any case, does not need a delegation to the MCC to have a military presence in the country, as noted above.

Perhaps Peru might send a few members of its civil guard.

63. *El Panamá-América,* December 26, 1997.

64. This is not a purely academic concern. Shortly before President George Bush's visit to Panama in 1992, two American soldiers were murdered in cold blood by Pedro Miguel González, son of the president of the Democratic Revolutionary Party. Despite eyewitnesses, no Panamanian court felt capable of establishing his guilt. *Miami Herald,* October 23, 1997.

65. *La Prensa,* March 24, 1997.

66. ANCAN dispatch, *Foreign Broadcast Information Service–Latin America,* August 16, 1996.

67. *El Siglo,* October 15, 1996.

68. One sign of this was the continued improvement of certain U.S. military facilities in the 1970s and 1980s.

69. U.S. Senate, *U.S. Military Presence,* p. 21.

CHAPTER 6: TOWARD 2000 AND AFTER

1. *El Panamá-América* (Panama City), March 26, 1996.

2. This was the view of the late Gabriel Lewis. As he explained it shortly before his death, the original concept was to replace American soldiers with Panamanian soldiers and thus make his country one of the nations "with the largest and best-equipped armies on the continent. With the pretext of defending the Canal, the familiar clan would have consolidated itself and democratic [rule] would have had no chance at all." *El Siglo* (Panama City), October 11, 1996.

3. James Kitfield, "Yankee, Don't Go!" *National Journal,* February 24, 1996.

4. Ibid.

5. James Kitfield, "Out of Panama," *Government Executive,* May 1996.

6. According to a news report, robberies and land seizures have become so common that the Panamanian authorities were forced to ask the Southern Command to resume joint patrols of the type that characterized the security situation shortly after the U.S. invasion in 1990. *El Panamá-América,* April 6, 1995.

7. *La Prensa* (Panama City), April 9, 1996.

8. No less a person than former president Nicolás Ardito Barletta has suggested that it would be desirable for the United States to consider delaying its departure from certain facilities for ten years after 2000 to ensure a smoother transition and also—he candidly admitted—to generate confidence on the part of foreign investors. *El Panamá-América,* October 15, 1995.

9. *La Estrella de Panamá* (Panama City), April 20, 1995.

10. *El Panamá-América,* August 6, 1991.

11. RPC-TV, *Foreign Broadcast Information Service—Latin America,* February 14, 1992.

12. Two exclusive residential areas of Panama City.

13. Alvaro Cabal Miranda in *El Panamá-América*, August 6, 1991.

14. Ibid., June 27, 1996.

15. Ibid., May 21, 1992.

16. Autoridad Regional Interoceánica, *Panama: The Investment Center of the Americas* (Panama City: ARI, 1995).

17. *El Panamá-América*, March 26, 1996. I am also basing this section on the oral presentation of President Barletta at the Council on Foreign Relations in New York, February 15, 1996.

18. It will now presumably be turned over to the multilateral counternarcotics center.

19. Ibid., February 18, 1996. The prospect of a presidential election, the return of the canal, and the withdrawal of the last American troops all occurring in the same year—1999—led Fernández to suggest that Panama's domestic tranquility would be better served if one of the three events was postponed.

20. Barletta told the staff delegation that a Korean-American firm had signed a contract to invest $300 million in these facilities over the next six years.

21. According to a recent report, The School of the Americas has just been acquired by a Spanish-Mexican consortium, "which plans to spend $20 million turning the decaying building into a five-star hotel catering to eco-tourists." *New York Times*, July 13, 1997.

22. U.S. Senate, Committee on Foreign Relations, *The Future of U.S. Military Presence in Panama*, 105th Cong., 1st sess., 1997, p. 31.

23. *La Estrella de Panamá*, July 9, 1996.

24. *Euromoney*, July 1996.

25. Although the base negotiations with the Philippines were followed with a certain degree of interest in the Panamanian press—with the $1 billion figure even bandied about as the size of a possible U.S. sweetener to remain in Panama—when the United States decided not to meet Manila's price but to withdraw altogether, the metaphor seems not to have registered on the Panamanians. Presumably, they comforted themselves with the thought that Panama was more important to the United States than the Philippines—either because it was closer, its people "whiter," or its location more strategically significant. In any event, the U.S. withdrawal from the Philippines in 1992 had no impact whatever in discouraging the Panamanians from seeking a compensation package in exchange for permitting the American military to remain.

26. *Los Angeles Times*, November 24, 1996.

27. *La Prensa*, October 20, 1994.

28. TVN Television Network, *Foreign Broadcast Information Service—Latin America*, August 30, 1996.

29. *La Prensa*, December 10, 1996. INTEL has nonetheless subsequently been privatized.

30. *Foreign Broadcast Information Service—Latin America*, August 27, 1990.

31. *Wall Street Journal,* October 17, 1997.

32. Nando net dispatch, November 17, 1995.

33. Ibid.

34. *Washington Times*, March 28, 1997.

35. U.S. Senate, *U.S. Military Presence.*

36. *New York Times*, September 28, 1997.

37. See, for example, a circular letter to potential foreign investors, dated July 25, 1997, that blurs the distinction between projects under discussion and contracts signed.

38. A piñata is a papier-mâché animal, normally a cow stuffed with toys and candy, which children in Latin American homes take turns trying to split with a stick, usually while blindfolded. The term *piñata* has come to mean a bonanza of patronage favors.

39. *New York Times*, July 13, 1997.

Index

---------------------★---------------------

About the Author

M ark Falcoff is a resident scholar at the American Enterprise Institute. He has taught at the Universities of Illinois, Oregon, and California, Los Angeles, as well as at the U.S. Foreign Service Institute. During the Ninety-ninth Congress, Mr. Falcoff served on the staff of the Senate Foreign Relations Committee.

His books include *Modern Chile, 1970–89: A Critical History; Small Countries, Large Issues* (also published by AEI); and *Searching for Panama* (with Richard Millett).

He received his M.A. and Ph.D. from Princeton University.

This book was edited by
Ann Petty of the publications staff
of the American Enterprise Institute.
The text was set in Bodoni.
Alice Anne English set the type,
and Edwards Brothers, Incorporated,
of Lillington, North Carolina,
printed and bound the book,
using permanent acid-free paper.

The AEI Press is the publisher for the American Enterprise Institute for Public Policy Research, 1150 Seventeenth Street, N.W., Washington, D.C. 20036; *Christopher DeMuth*, publisher; *Dana Lane*, director; *Ann Petty*, editor; *Leigh Tripoli*, editor; *Cheryl Weissman*, editor; *Alice Anne English*, production manager.